Editor
Eric Migliaccio

Illustrator
Mark Mason

Cover Artist
Brenda DiAntonis

Editor in Chief
Ina Massler Levin, M.A.

Creative Director
Karen J. Goldfluss, M.S. Ed.

Art Production Manager
Kevin Barnes

Art Coordinator
Renée Christine Yates

Imaging
Rosa C. See

Publisher

Mary D. Smith, M.S. Ed.

Content Area Lessons Using **Graphic Organizers**

Grade 6

- Teach content and thought processes simultaneously
- Promote inferential and evaluative thinking
- Improve critical and analytical thinking skills
- Enhance cross-curricular understandings

CD-ROM

Teacher Created Resources

Author

Debra J. Housel, M.S. Ed.

Teacher Created Resources, Inc.
6421 Industry Way
Westminster, CA 92683
www.teachercreated.com

ISBN: 978-1-4206-8096-6

© 2008 Teacher Created Resources, Inc.
Made in U.S.A.

Teacher Created Resources

Table of Contents

Introduction

Content Area Lessons Using Graphic Organizers is designed to save you time and effort. It contains complete lessons that meet the standards for your grade level in reading, writing, science, geography, history, and math. Each lesson uses a different graphic organizer. Thus, if you do all the lessons in this book and never use another graphic organizer, your students will have worked with 23 different graphic organizers. This provides significant exposure to these important educational tools.

Graphic organizers show the organization of concepts and the relationships among them. They offer a clear depiction of data, which research has proven is more memorable than pages of notes. They show students "how it all fits together," which is much more effective than having them try to memorize bits of data without thoroughly understanding the context. Showing how information is organized helps students—especially English-language learners and those with reading disabilities—focus on content instead of semantics and grammar.

Compelling Reasons to Use Graphic Organizers

Research shows that graphic organizers actually improve students' creative, analytical, and critical-thinking skills. Why? Graphic organizers help students of all ages to process information. Processing information is a complex skill requiring the ability to identify essential ideas; decide which details are relevant and which are irrelevant; understand how information is structured; and perhaps most importantly of all, figure out how data relates to other information or situations. Processing information demands the use of such higher-level thinking skills as making decisions, drawing conclusions, and forming inferences.

Substantial amounts of research support the fact that graphic organizers increase the understanding and retention of critical information for students who range from gifted to those with learning disabilities. This means that using graphic organizers may meet the needs of the many different learners in your classroom without the time-consuming task of individualization.

The visual element inherent in graphic organizers supports three cognitive learning theories: dual coding theory, schema theory, and cognitive load theory.

- **Dual coding theory** acknowledges that presenting information in both visual and verbal form improves recall and recognition. Graphic organizers do both effectively.

- **Schema theory** states that a learner's prediction based on his or her background knowledge (schema) is crucial for acquiring new information. This is why readers have a hard time comprehending material in an unfamiliar subject even when they know the meaning of the separate words in the text. Graphic organizers' ability to show relationships builds upon and increases students' schema.

- **Cognitive load theory** stresses that a student's short-term memory has limitations in the amount of data it can simultaneously hold. Since any instructional information must first be processed by short-term memory, for long-term memory (schema acquisition) to occur, instruction must reduce the short-term memory load. Thus, teaching methods that cut down on the demands of short-term memory give the brain a better opportunity to facilitate activation of long-term memory. Graphic organizers fit the bill perfectly.

Graphic organizers are appearing more often in standardized tests and state assessments. Giving your students practice with the variety of graphic organizers offered in this book can help them to achieve better scores on these assessments.

Introduction *(cont.)*

How to Use This Book

Each lesson in *Content Area Lessons Using Graphic Organizers* is designed to be used where it fits into your curriculum. Whenever you start a new unit, check to see if one of these lessons will work with your topic. Where applicable, reading levels based on the Flesch-Kincaid formula are included.

The lessons often require that you make a transparency and student copies of the graphic organizers located on the CD. Any other necessary materials will be stated in the lesson. These might include such things as highlighters, index cards, poster board, scissors, glue, and zipper bags. If possible, when writing on the overhead transparency, use different colors to differentiate between specific sections. This is another way to help your students to visualize data.

The graphic organizers give as much space as possible for the students to write. However, if some of your students have large handwriting, make an overhead transparency of the blank graphic organizer and display it on the overhead. Then have a school aide or the students tape a sheet of construction paper where the overhead projects and copy the format onto the paper. This will give them more room to write.

If you are just starting to use graphic organizers, you may worry that they are time-consuming. Keep in mind that it is time well spent. Graphic organizers provide meaningful instruction that gives your students an advantage in comprehending and remembering data. By using graphic organizers you are teaching not just content but thought processes. Your students are learning how to learn—an invaluable skill that will serve them well for the rest of their lives.

Be Flexible and Creative

The graphic organizers included in *Content Area Lessons Using Graphic Organizers* have many uses; they are not limited to the lessons or subject area in which they appear. Most of these graphic organizers can be used or modified to fit the needs of other lessons or subjects. Sometimes a student will self-advocate by asking you to make copies of a certain kind for use in other areas. You may find that a challenged student enjoys and learns best using one particular type. Be flexible and creative in your use of graphic organizers.

If you have a class that really enjoys graphic organizers, you could opt to evaluate student learning by letting the students create their own graphic organizers. You may be pleasantly surprised by your students' abilities to make meaningful graphics that show interrelationships in a more effective way than they could explain in writing.

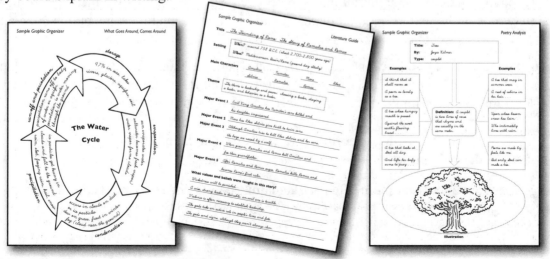

Standards Correlation Chart

Each lesson in this book meets at least one of the following standards and benchmarks, which are used with permission from McREL. Copyright 2006 McREL. Mid-continent Research for Education and Learning. 2250 S. Parker Road, Suite 500. Aurora, CO 80014. Telephone: 303-337-0990. Website: *www.mcrel.org/standards-benchmarks*

Standards and Benchmarks	Pages
Math	
Standard 2. Understands and applies basic and advanced properties of the concepts of numbers	
• **Benchmark 1.** Understands the relationships among equivalent number representations and the advantages and disadvantages of each type of representation	14–16
Standard 3. Uses basic and advanced procedures while performing the processes of computation	
• **Benchmark 5.** Uses proportional reasoning to solve mathematical and real-world problems (e.g., involving equivalent fractions, decimals, percents)	11–13
Standard 5. Understands and applies basic and advanced properties of the concepts of geometry	
• **Benchmark 2.** Understands the defining properties of triangles	8–10
Science	
Standard 1. Understands atmospheric processes and the water cycle	
• **Benchmark 2.** Knows the processes involved in the water cycle (e.g., evaporation, condensation, precipitation, surface run-off, percolation) and their effects on climatic patterns	21–24
• **Benchmark 3.** Knows that the Sun is the principal energy source for phenomena on the Earth's surface (e.g., winds, ocean currents, the water cycle, plant growth)	17–24
• **Benchmark 6.** Knows ways in which clouds affect weather and climate (e.g., precipitation, reflection of light from the Sun, retention of heat energy emitted from the Earth's surface)	21–24
Standard 4. Understands the principles of heredity and related concepts	
• **Benchmark 1.** Knows that reproduction is a characteristic of all living things and is essential to the continuation of a species	25–29
• **Benchmark 3.** Understands asexual and sexual reproduction (e.g., in asexual reproduction, all the genes come from a single parent; in sexual reproduction, an egg and sperm unite and half of the genes come from each parent, so the offspring is never identical to either of its parents; sexual reproduction allows for greater genetic diversity; asexual reproduction limits the spread of disadvantageous characteristics through a species)	25–29
Standard 8. Understands the structure and properties of matter	
• **Benchmark 1.** Knows that matter is made up of tiny particles called atoms, and different arrangements of atoms into groups compose all substances	30–33
Standard 9. Understands the sources and properties of energy	
• **Benchmark 1.** Knows that energy is a property of many substances (e.g., electrical energy is in the attraction or repulsion between charges)	30–33
• **Benchmark 5.** Knows that electrical circuits provide a means of transferring electrical energy to produce heat, light, sound, and chemical changes	30–33
Standard 10. Understands forces and motion	
• **Benchmark 2.** Knows that just as electric currents can produce magnetic forces, magnets can cause electrical currents	30–33
World History	
Standard 3. Understands the major characteristics of civilization and the development of civilizations in Mesopotamia, Egypt, and the Indus Valley	
• **Benchmark 1.** Understands influences on the development of various civilizations in the 4th and 3rd millennia BCE (e.g., how the natural environment of the Tigris-Euphrates, Nile, and Indus Valleys shaped the early development of civilization; characteristics of urban development in Mesopotamia, Egypt, and the Indus Valley)	34–38
• **Benchmark 3.** Understands how economic, political, and environmental factors influenced the civilizations of Mesopotamia, Egypt, and the Indus Valley (e.g., the importance of commercial, cultural, and political connections between Egypt and peoples of Nubia along the upper Nile; how geography and climate affected trade in the Nile Valley)	34–38
Standard 8. Understands how Aegean civilization emerged and how interrelations developed among peoples of the Eastern Mediterranean and Southwest Asia from 600 to 200 BCE	
• **Benchmark 2.** Understands the major cultural elements of Greek society (e.g., how Greek gods and goddesses represent non-human entities, and how gods, goddesses, and humans interact in Greek myths)	65–68

Standards Correlation Chart *(cont.)*

Standards and Benchmarks	Pages
World History *(cont.)*	
Standard 9. Understands how major religious and large-scale empires arose in the Mediterranean Basin, China, and India from 500 BCE to 300 CE	
• **Benchmark 1.** Understand the origins and social framework of Roman society (e.g., how legends about the founding of Rome describe ancient Rome and reflect the beliefs and values of its citizens)	39–42
• **Benchmark 7.** Understands the origins of Buddhism and fundamental Buddhist beliefs (e.g., the life story of Buddha and his essential teachings; how the Buddhist teachings were a response to the Brahmanic system)	47–52
Standard 13. Understands the causes and consequences of the development of Islamic civilization between the 7th and 10th centuries	
• **Benchmark 1.** Understands the spread of Islam in Southwest Asia and the Mediterranean region	61–64
• **Benchmark 2.** Understands the influence of Islamic ideas and practices on other cultures and social behavior	61–64
Standard 23. Understands patterns of crisis and recovery in Afro-Eurasia between 1300 and 1450	
• **Benchmark 1.** Understands the origins and impact of the plague (e.g., how the plague started and spread across Eurasia and North Africa; the impact of the plague on daily life in urban Southwest Asia and Europe; how the plague changed the lives of survivors)	43–46
Geography	
Standard 1. Understands the characteristics and uses of maps, globes, and other geographic tools and technologies	
• **Benchmark 3.** Understands concepts such as axis, seasons, rotation, and revolution (Earth-Sun relations)	53–56
Standard 2. Knows the location of places, geographic features, and patterns of the environment	
• **Benchmark 1.** Knows the location of physical and human features on maps and globes (e.g., major ocean currents; wind patterns; land forms; climate regions)	53–56
Standard 3. Understands the characteristics and uses of spatial organization of Earth's surface	
• **Benchmark 4.** Understands the patterns and processes of migration and diffusion (e.g., the spread of language, religion, and customs from one culture to another; spread of a contagious disease through a population)	43–46
Standard 4. Understands the physical and human characteristics of place	
• **Benchmark 1.** Knows the human characteristics of places (e.g., cultural characteristics such as religion, language, politics, technology, family structure, gender; population characteristics; land uses; levels of development)	47–52, 61–64
Standard 5. Understands the concept of regions	
• **Benchmark 1.** Knows regions at various spatial scales (e.g., hemispheres, regions within continents, countries, cities)	53–56
Standard 6. Understands that culture and experience influence people's perceptions of places and regions.	
• **Benchmark 1.** Knows how places and regions serve as cultural symbols	53–56
• **Benchmark 3.** Knows the ways in which culture influences the perception of places and regions (e.g., religion and other belief systems, language and tradition; perceptions of "beautiful" or "valuable")	61–64
Standard 7. Knows the physical processes that shape patterns on Earth's surface	
• **Benchmark 2.** Knows the processes that produce renewable and nonrenewable resources (e.g., fossil fuels, hydroelectric power)	30–33
Standard 8. Understands the characteristics of ecosystems on Earth's surface	
• **Benchmark 3.** Understands ecosystems in terms of their characteristics and ability to withstand stress caused by physical events (e.g., regrowth of a forest after a forest fire)	57–60
Standard 18. Understands global development and environmental issues	
• **Benchmark 1.** Understands how the interaction between physical and human systems affects current conditions on Earth (e.g., relationships involved in economic, political, social, and environmental changes; global warming impact of using petroleum, coal, nuclear power, and solar power as major energy sources)	57–60

Standards Correlation Chart *(cont.)*

Standards and Benchmarks	Pages
Language Arts Reading	
Standard 6. Uses reading skills and strategies to understand and interpret a variety of literary texts	
• **Benchmark 1.** Uses reading skills and strategies to understand a variety of literary passages and texts	65–68, 73-76
• **Benchmark 2.** Knows the defining characteristics of a variety of literary forms and genres	65–68, 73-76
• **Benchmark 6.** Understands the use of language in literary works to convey mood, images, and meaning (e.g., voice; alliteration; onomatopoeia; figurative language such as similes, metaphors, personification, hyperbole, allusion)	69–72
Standard 7. Uses reading skills and strategies to understand and interpret a variety of informational texts	
• **Benchmark 1.** Uses reading skills and strategies to understand a variety of informational texts (e.g., electronic texts; textbooks; biographical sketches; directions; essays; primary source historical documents, including letters and diaries; print media, including editorials, news stories, periodicals, and magazines)	77–92
• **Benchmark 2.** Knows the defining characteristics of a variety of informational texts (e.g., electronic texts; textbooks; biographical sketches; letters; diaries; directions; procedures; magazines; essays; primary source historical documents; editorials; news stories; periodicals)	77–84
• **Benchmark 7.** Differentiates between fact and opinion in informational texts	77–84
Language Arts Writing	
Standard 1. Uses the general skills and strategies of the writing process	
• **Benchmark 5.** Uses content, style, and structure (e.g., formal or informal language, genre, organization) appropriate for specific audiences and purposes (e.g., to entertain, to influence, to inform)	81–84
• **Benchmark 10.** Writes persuasive compositions (e.g., engages the reader by establishing a context, creating a persona, and otherwise developing reader interest; develops a controlling idea that conveys a judgment; creates and organizes a structure appropriate to the needs and interests of a specific audience; arranges details, reasons, examples, and/or anecdotes persuasively; excludes information and arguments that are irrelevant; anticipates and addresses reader concerns and counter arguments; supports arguments with detailed evidence)	81–84
• **Benchmark 11.** Writes compositions that address problems/solutions (e.g., identifies and defines a problem in a way appropriate to the intended audience, describes at least one solution, presents logical and well-supported reasons)	81–84
Standard 2. Uses the stylistic and rhetorical aspects of writing	
• **Benchmark 3.** Uses a variety of sentence structures to expand and embed ideas	85–88
• **Benchmark 4.** Uses explicit transitional devices	85–88
Standard 3. Uses grammatical and mechanical conventions in written compositions	
• **Benchmark 6.** Uses adjectives in written compositions	93–96
• **Benchmark 10** Uses conventions of spelling in written compositions (e.g., uses compounds, roots, suffixes, prefixes, and syllable constructions to spell words)	93–96
Standard 4. Gathers and uses information for research purposes	
• **Benchmark 4.** Uses a variety of resource materials to gather information for research topics (e.g., magazines, newspapers, dictionaries, journals, phone directories, globes, atlases, almanacs, technological sources)	81–84 89–92
• **Benchmark 5.** Determines the appropriateness of an information source for a research topic	81–84, 89-92
• **Benchmark 7.** Writes research papers	89–92
• **Benchmark 8.** Uses appropriate methods to cite and document reference sources	89–92

Math

Day 1

1. Prior to this lesson, your students must understand acute, right, and obtuse angles, as well as acute, right, scalene, obtuse, and isosceles triangles.

2. Make an overhead transparency and copies of the "Laying Tiles" graphic organizer on page 10. Obtain clear number tiles (or cut out the ones on your transparency) to use on the overhead.

3. Have your students cut out the individual number tiles on the page.

4. Have students glue their tile boards to a piece of poster board and store their number tiles in a zipper bag.

5. Working as a class, solve the first two problems together and have a student come up and display the correct answer on the overhead. Tell the students to place the tiles, moving from top to bottom.

6. Say, "Now we are going to use each tile once. I will ask a question about angles or triangles, and you will place the tiles. Do not shout out the answer. If you don't know one, skip it. We'll go over it." Repeat each question twice, being sure to give enough time for students to think.

7. Ask these questions: How many degrees are in a straight angle? (*180°*) How many degrees is in an angle that is half as large as a right angle? (*45°*) How many sides are equal in an isosceles triangle? (*2*) Two of a scalene triangle's angles add up to 143 degrees. How many degrees are in the third angle? (*37°*) How could the numbers you have left form the number of degrees in an obtuse angle. (*96°—only those two digits were left, and 69 is an acute angle.*)

8. Go over the answers, asking individual students to explain how they determined the right answer. Have the students clear their boards.

9. Repeat the procedure, but this time have students work independently. Afterwards, have a student come up and display the correct answer on the overhead. Ask these questions: How many degrees are in each acute angle of a right isosceles triangle? (*45°*) A scalene triangle has how many unequal sides? (*3*) Two angles in an acute triangle total 113 degrees. How many degrees are in the third angle? (*67°*) How many total degrees in an isosceles triangle? (*180°*) Look at the digits you have left. Arrange the digits to form the degrees of the largest angle in an obtuse triangle. How do you know? (*92°—only those two digits were left; 29 is acute, and an obtuse triangle's largest angle must have one angle more than 90 degrees*)

Days 2–5

1. Have students get out their tile boards and number tiles.

2. Repeat the activity above using a variety of pre-prepared triangle and angle questions.

Next Week

1. Have students get out their tile boards and number tiles.

2. Pair the students. They must place all 10 digits in any order and then write appropriate triangle and angle questions next to each number. This is challenging because the children must generate the questions and can use each digit only once.

3. Have each pair write their number sentences and answers on a piece of paper to turn in.

4. If your class enjoys this activity, you can have them do it again independently.

Note: These are the answers for the questions given in step 9 on page 8.

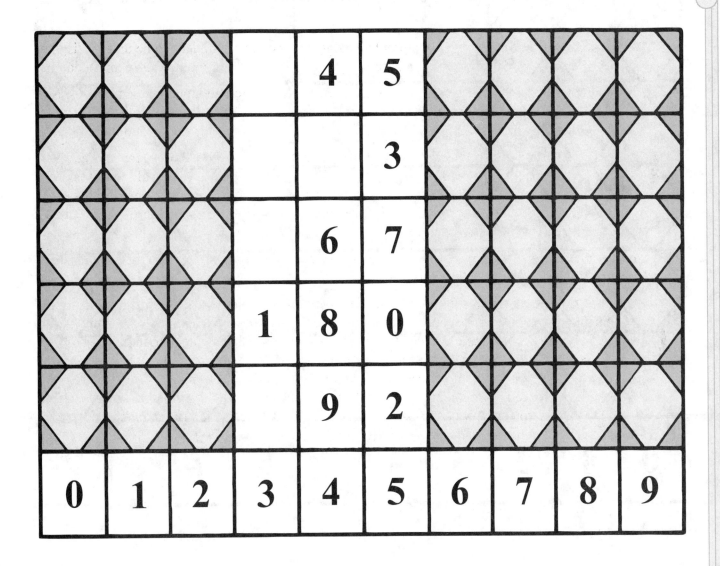

Math

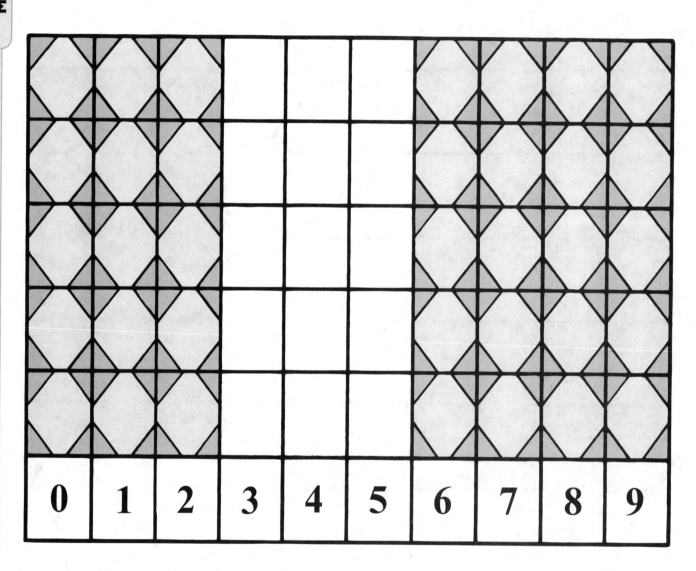

1. Prior to this lesson, your students must be familiar with percentages and their relationship to decimals.

2. Make an overhead transparency and copies of the "Follow the Steps" graphic organizer on page 13.

3. Write this word problem at the top of your transparency:

> *Jack sees a leather coat on sale for $157. A sign states: "Take an additional 20% off the lowest ticket price." What is the sale price of the coat?*

4. Working as a class, guide the students through the steps to solve the problem:

   - *Identify:* Coat is $157. There's an extra 20% off. What's the final price?

   - *Decide:* Do one of the following:

   Change the 20% to a decimal (.20) and multiply it times $157. "Off" means "take away," so subtract the amount from $157.

   Take the complement of 20% (80%), change it to a decimal (.80), and multiply it times $157 (this will save the subtraction step).

   - *Solve:* $157 x .20 = $31.40; $157 − 31.40 = $125.60

   - *Check:* $31.40 ÷ .20 = $157; $125.60 + 31.40 = $157

5. Explain that this is the not actual price that Jack will pay. He must pay sales tax, too. Show your students how to determine the final cost by multiplying the $125.60 x 1.XX (use your local sales tax—for example, 7.5% sales tax would be converted to 1.075). The 1 covers the base price and the .075 covers the sales tax. The alternative way is to convert the sales tax to a decimal, multiply it by $125.60, and then add the result to $125.60 to get the total cost.

6. Depending on the needs of your class, do the next word problem as a whole class, in pairs, or independently:

> *A restaurant can hold 135 patrons. The owner's goal is to have the restaurant at least 70% full during each dinner hour (5 p.m. to 8 p.m.). How many patrons does the owner hope to serve in one night? Round to the nearest whole person.*

   - *Identify:* Full capacity is 135. Must find 70% of that for each of three hours (5:00, 6:00, and 7:00).

   - *Decide:* Change 70 to a decimal and multiply by 135. Then multiply by 3 hours.

   - *Solve:* 135 x .70 = 94.5 x 3 = 283.5; rounded to 284 patrons

   - *Check:* 283.5 ÷ 3 = 94.5 ÷ .70 = 135

7. Discuss the importance of rounding to the nearest whole person (since there are no half persons).

8. Use this graphic organizer with any word problems. You can make more copies of the blank "Follow the Steps" graphic organizer or have the student refer to the steps while doing them on a separate sheet of paper.

Note: The "Follow the Steps" graphic organizer can be used as a sequencing organizer in any subject area if you cover the words on the steps and in the boxes before you make copies.

Note: These are the answers to the first word problem given on page 11.

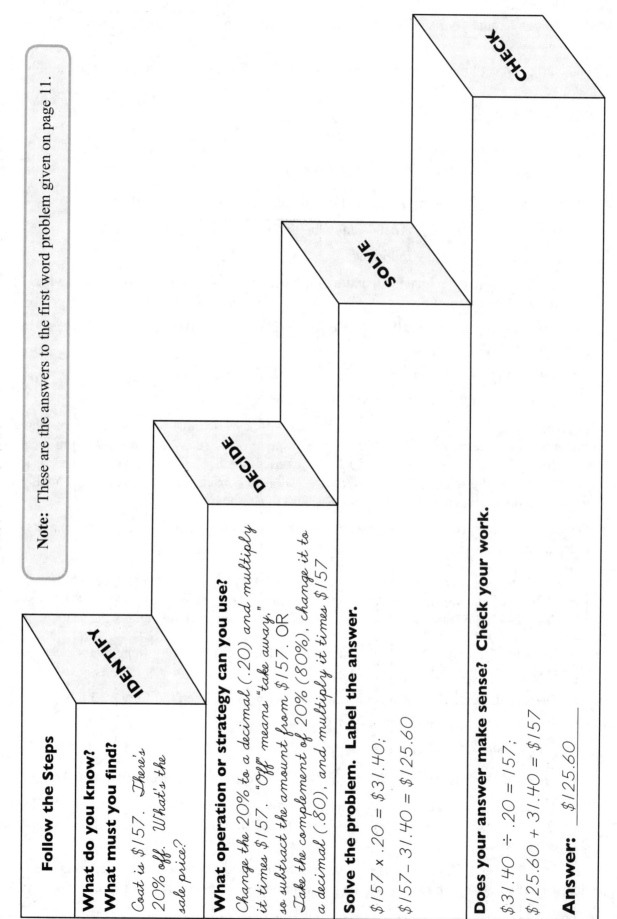

Follow the Steps

IDENTIFY

What do you know?
What must you find?

Coat is $157. There's 20% off. What's the sale price?

DECIDE

What operation or strategy can you use?

Change the 20% to a decimal (.20) and multiply it times $157. "Off" means "take away," so subtract the amount from $157. OR Take the complement of 20% (80%), change it to a decimal (.80), and multiply it times $157

SOLVE

Solve the problem. Label the answer.

$157 × .20 = $31.40;

$157 − 31.40 = $125.60

CHECK

Does your answer make sense? Check your work.

$31.40 ÷ .20 = 157;

$125.60 + 31.40 = $157

Answer: *$125.60* _____

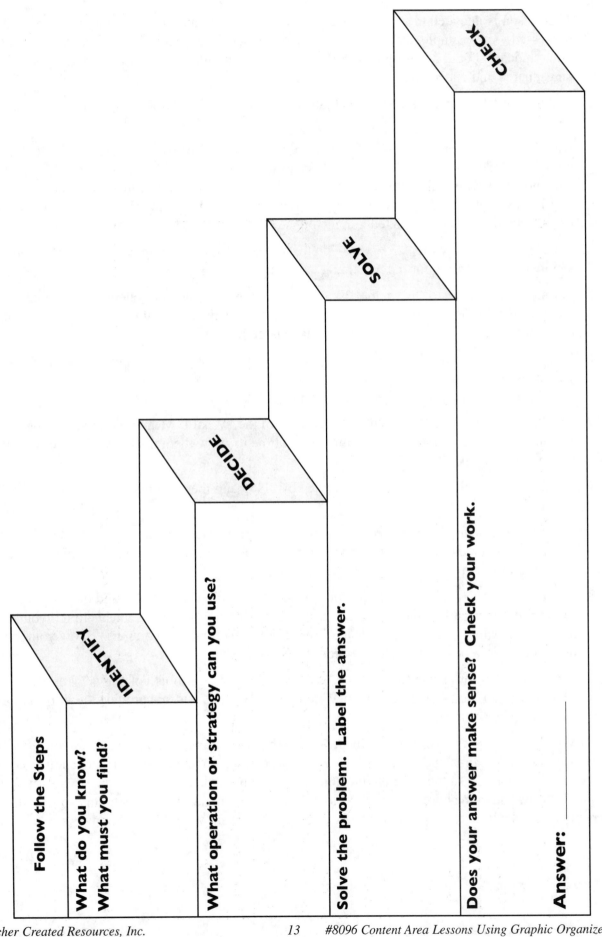

Follow the Steps

What do you know?
What must you find?

What operation or strategy can you use?

Solve the problem. Label the answer.

Does your answer make sense? Check your work.

Answer: _____

1. This lesson is intended to solidify your students' understanding of how numbers are related and expressed—for example, that 1/2 can also be expressed as .5 and 50%. Prior to doing this lesson, your students should be familiar with fractions, mixed numbers, decimals, percentages, sales tax, and squared and cubed numbers.

2. Make an overhead transparency and student copies of the "It's All Relative" graphic organizer on page 16.

3. Distribute the copies and display the transparency. Write "75%" in the "Expression" column while the students do so at their seats. Ask the students to explain what it means (75 out of 100) and another way in which it can be expressed (.75 or 3/4). Challenge them to come up with a real-life example. One is provided for you in the completed graphic organizer on page 15. Use the information in the completed graphic organizer if your class gets stumped.

4. For the second row, write "23 ÷ 1,000" in the "What It Means" column. See if the students can supply the information for the remaining columns.

5. For the third row, write "8²" in the "Expression" column and ask the students to volunteer the information for the rest of the columns in the row. This is a great opportunity to clear up misunderstandings students may have about squared numbers.

6. In the fourth row, write "five-eighths" in the "What It Means" column and ask the students to volunteer the information for the rest of the columns in the row. Be sure to take time to clear up misconceptions that you may discover when the students volunteer answers.

7. For the fifth row, write "8.65 cents of every $1" in the "What It Means" column. Guide your students to fill in the rest of the columns. Take time to show them that there are two ways to figure out sales tax:

   • They can multiply the item's base price by .0865 and then add that number to the item's base price.

   • They can save a step by multiplying the item's base price by 1.0865. Make certain that they understand that the "1" is there to account for the item's base price, while the decimal accounts for the sales tax percentage.

8. For the sixth row, write "There were four pizzas cut into five slices each, and the kids at the party ate 3 ⁴/₅ of the pizzas" in the "Real-Life Example" column. Ask your students to tell you how much pizza is left (*one slice*). Then ask how to fill in the first two columns. Show your students how to convert a mixed number to a decimal and percentage.

9. For the seventh row, write "The square box has sides of 4 cm, so its volume is 64 cubic centimeters" in the "Real-Life Example" column. Have the students provide the information for the rest of the columns.

Extension: Write these words on the board or overhead: *percent, decimal, fraction, mixed number, improper number, ratio,* and *exponential number.* Then pair students and distribute another copy of the graphic organizer to them. Have them generate seven numbers that they can explain, express in another way, and come up with a real-world example for. This will be challenging, so pair stronger math students with weaker ones. Don't expect the variety that you provided them.

Sample Graphic Organizer

It's All Relative

Math

Expression	What It It Means	Can Also Be Expressed As	Real-Life Example
75%	75 out of 100	.75 $\frac{3}{4}$	75% of the students turned in their homework.
.023	$23 \div 1,000$	2.3% $\frac{23}{1,000}$	Last year, .023 of the 100,000 packages were lost—or 2,300
8^2	8 squared, or 8×8	64	The garden was 8 yards by 8 yards, so it had an area of 64 square yards.
$\frac{5}{8}$	five-eighths (5 parts of something that is split into 8 parts)	.625 62.5%	The dress only had $\frac{5}{8}$ of its buttons, so 3 were missing.
8.65% sales tax	8,65 cents of every $1	.0865	Multiply $100 item by 1.0865 to find out the item will really cost you $108.65.
$3\frac{4}{5}$	3 whole and 4 of 5 parts	3.80 or 380%	There were four pizzas cut into five slices each, and the kids at the party ate $3\frac{4}{5}$ of the pizzas. Just one piece is left.
4^3	4 cubed	$4 \times 4 \times 4$	The square box has sides of 4 cm, so its volume is 64 cubic centimeters.

©Teacher Created Resources, Inc.

15

#8096 Content Area Lessons Using Graphic Organizers

Math

Expression	What It It Means	Can Also Be Expressed As	Real-Life Example

1. Write the word *wind* on the board. Give students 30 seconds to write what they know about the topic. This writing will not be shared, but it lets students approach the reading with confidence by making them realize they already know something about the topic.

2. Introduce any unfamiliar vocabulary:
   ✧ **catalyst**—something that causes a reaction or event to occur
   ✧ **prevailing**—common; frequent; predominant
   ✧ **doldrums**—a region in the Atlantic Ocean where wind is scarce
   ✧ **wind shear**—an abrupt change in wind direction and speed, especially a sudden strong downdraft

3. Make student copies of "Windy Weather" on page 18. It is written at a 6.4 reading level. Have your students take turns reading aloud each paragraph.

4. Stop after the first paragraph has been read and ask:
   • From what direction would the wind probably be blowing to bring in warmer air? (*south*) How about colder air? (*north*)
   • How does the sun make the wind blow? (*Do not confirm or deny the answer; you just want them to make a prediction.*)

5. Stop after the second paragraph has been read and ask:
   • Why do predictable wind patterns form? (*Due to Earth's tilt, the sun always heats the central part (equator) the same amount year 'round.*)
   • Where do you think the trade winds are located? (*Do not confirm or deny the answer; you just want them to make a prediction.*)

6. Stop after the fourth paragraph has been read and ask:
   • Centuries ago why couldn't sailors do anything about being stuck in the doldrums? (*Wind moved their ships, and there is no wind in the doldrums.*)
   • Think about the doldrums. Where do you think the trade winds are located? (*more than 700 miles away on both sides of the equator*)
   • In what direction is a northwest wind blowing? (*south and east—it's coming from the north and west*)

7. Stop after reading the sixth paragraph and ask:
   • At what level in the atmosphere are the winds on the Beaufort Scale measured? (*near the ground*) What is used to measure them? (*usually an anemometer*)
   • What is the difference between a tornado and a microburst? (*Although both are caused by wind shear, a tornado is a spinning funnel cloud, and a microburst is a strong sudden downdraft. Since a microburst does not travel, all its damage is directly beneath it, while a tornado leaves a damage path.*)

8. Make an overhead transparency and student copies of the organizer on page 20.

9. Complete the organizer as a class. First, decide on the main idea. Do this at the board as students give you information that they think should be incorporated into the main idea. Combine their ideas until you have something similar to the main idea shown on the canal on the completed graphic organizer on page 19.

10. On the windmill tower itself, have your students write the information about the wind-measurement scales mentioned in the passage. Then ask students to give the most important facts from the article to write on the windmill's eight blades.

Science

Windy Weather

You know that wind is air moving across Earth's surface. You know that a dry day can turn soggy if wind brings in a rainstorm and that a cool day will heat up if wind blows from a warmer area. But do you know what causes the wind to blow? The sun! In fact, the sun is the catalyst for most of Earth's weather.

The sun heats Earth's surface and its atmosphere, but it does not heat them evenly. The air above Earth's hot areas rises into the atmosphere. Air from a colder area flows in to replace the heated air. This air movement, called circulation, causes predictable winds to form over large parts of Earth. These prevailing winds change with latitude. Over the equator heated air rises high rapidly. Near the surface, cooler air rushes in to replace it, forming the trade winds. (Sailors once used these winds to their advantage when navigating their ships.) These trade winds do not blow straight toward the equator; they blow at an angle due to Earth's rotation.

However, near the equator and for about 700 miles (1,100 km) on either side of it, there are no prevailing winds. For centuries, sailors cursed this calm region called the doldrums. They would swelter under the sun's glare for days or weeks waiting for their ship to drift into a favorable ocean current or an area that had some wind.

Winds are named based on the direction from which they blow. A southeast wind blows from the south and east toward the north and west. Prevailing west winds move weather from west to east across the northern United States and southern Canada.

British Navy Admiral Francis Beaufort designed a wind scale in 1805. It goes from "no wind" to "hurricane" (sustained winds of 73 miles per hour or more). Near Earth's surface, wind speed is measured with an anemometer. This instrument has cups attached to spokes on a turning shaft. When the wind moves the spokes, the shaft turns. The speed of the spinning shaft tells the wind speed. Weather balloons and satellites help to determine wind speeds over the oceans. They measure the strength of hurricanes as they approach land. The Saffir-Simpson Hurricane Scale classifies hurricanes as Category 1 to 5, with 5 having the highest winds and causing the worst damage.

During thunderstorms, wind shear can cause microbursts or tornadoes. Microbursts are sudden, strong winds that flatten things—such as trees and buildings—directly beneath them. They occur without warning. The funnel cloud of a tornado gives slightly more warning. However, a tornado cannot be classified until after it is over. Tornadoes are rated F0 to F5 on the Fujita Scale based on the amount of damage that they cause. Scientists once believed that microbursts were short-lived tornadoes. However, a microburst does not travel, so all of its damage is in a straight line directly beneath the downdraft. A tornado leaves a path of damage as it roars across the ground.

Science

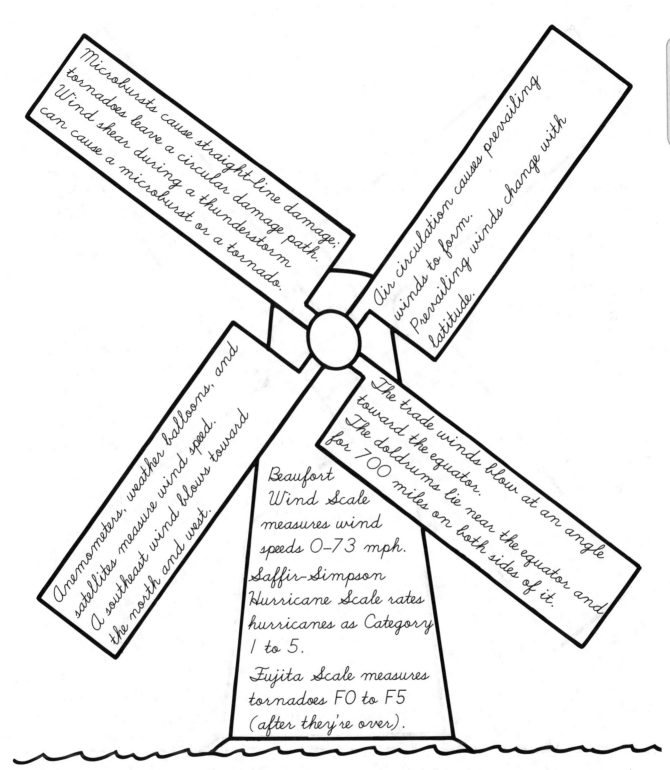

Microbursts cause straight-line damage. tornadoes leave a circular damage path. Wind shear during a thunderstorm can cause a microburst or a tornado.

Air circulation causes prevailing winds to form. Prevailing winds change with latitude.

Anemometers, weather balloons, and satellites measure wind speed. A southeast wind blows toward the north and west.

The trade winds blow at an angle toward the equator. The doldrums lie near the equator and for 700 miles on both sides of it.

Beaufort Wind Scale measures wind speeds 0–73 mph. Saffir-Simpson Hurricane Scale rates hurricanes as Category 1 to 5. Fujita Scale measures tornadoes F0 to F5 (after they're over).

The sun's uneven heating of Earth's surface and atmosphere causes wind, since warm air rises and cooler air moves in to replace it.

Science

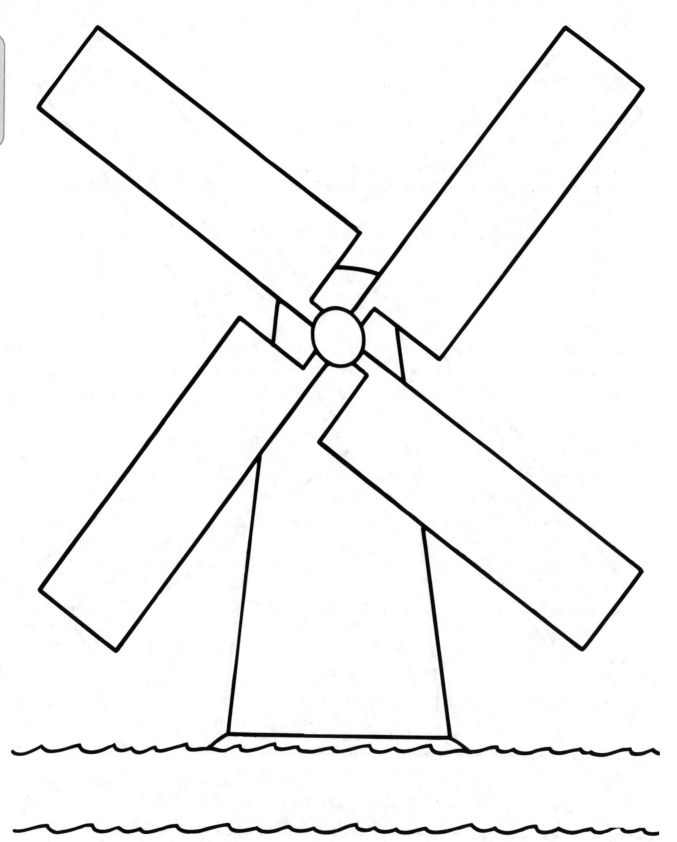

1. Draw a cycle diagram with four boxes on the board or overhead. Introduce the concept of natural cycles by asking students to tell you the seasons in order. Ask them if it matters which box each one goes in. (*The answer is yes and no. That's because the seasons must always go in the same order—for example, you can't have spring before winter—yet it doesn't matter which one you start with.*)

2. Ask students to think of another natural cycle (*phases of the moon; daylight/nighttime cycle; life cycle of any animal or human, etc.*). Guide them to see that although the steps must stay in order, the "first" step is indefinite, as the cycle continues over and over again. (*Which came first—the chicken or the egg?*)

3. Write this fact on the board: "Earth has so much water on it that water could cover the continental (*lower 48*) United States with a layer 92 miles deep!" Use this as a springboard to discuss these questions:

   • Where did all the water come from? (*Earth is a closed system; all that water has always been here. The forces that created Earth also created all the water.*)

   • Can it ever be used up? (*No. Earth recycles its water in the hydrologic, or water, cycle. Every drop of water on Earth has gone through this cycle many times.*)

   • Is most of Earth's water fresh or salty? (*Salty—97 percent of all water is seawater.*)

   • Which kind of water can we and other animals drink? (*Fresh—saltwater actually dehydrates and eventually kills because it causes individual cells to release water.*)

4. Make student copies of "The Water Cycle" on page 22. It is written at a 6.0 reading level.

5. Introduce any unfamiliar vocabulary

   ✧ **glacial**—having to do with a glacier

   ✧ **aquifer**— a geological formation like an underground reservoir containing ground water, especially one that supplies the water for wells and natural springs

   ✧ **evaporation**—the conversion of moisture into a vapor; boiling water causes evaporation, as the water turns into steam

   ✧ **condensation**—the process by which atmospheric water vapor liquefies to form fog, clouds, dew, frost, or precipitation

   ✧ **percolation**— the slow movement of water through soil or the pores in permeable (able to be passed through) rock

6. Have your students read the passage.

7. Make an overhead transparency and two copies for each student of the "What Goes Around, Comes Around" graphic organizer on page 24.

8. Display the transparency and distribute the copies. Fill in the organizer together.

9. As a class, write the words "The Water Cycle" in the center of the arrowed area. Then write each step of the water cycle above an arrow and the explanation inside the arrow.

10. Distribute the second set of student graphic organizers. For homework, have your students draw a picture to match each step inside the arrow and write the label for the step above the arrow.

Science

The Water Cycle

Water covers more than 70 percent of Earth's surface. This water can never be used up. Why? It moves through the water cycle over and over. Every drop of water has gone through this cycle—some of it billions of times. Right now each water molecule is somewhere in this cycle:

Storage

About 97 percent of all water lies in the oceans. Water is also stored in lakes, rivers, rocks, soil, and glaciers. Most glacial water stays frozen for hundreds of years. Water may also pool in underground reservoirs called aquifers. Aquifers are found in the first 10 miles of Earth's crust. Water below this depth can only get to the surface during a volcanic eruption.

Evaporation

Evaporation is the process by which liquid water changes into water vapor. It's what makes puddles dry up. The sun makes water evaporate from Earth's soil and surface water. Seawater is salty, but when it evaporates, it leaves the salt behind. Water vapor rises into the air. Clouds form when this vapor condenses or freezes onto tiny dust or ice pieces. These ice crystals are so small that they float. Winds blow the clouds around, so they pick up water in one area and drop it in another.

Condensation

Condensation does not just occur inside clouds. You have seen condensation as dew, frost, or fog. Dew forms when water vapor condenses as droplets onto a surface near the ground. If it is cold and water vapor condenses into ice crystals, then frost covers surfaces near the ground. Fog is essentially a cloud that is at ground level.

Precipitation

Precipitation occurs when water droplets or ice crystals inside a cloud get so heavy that they fall to the ground. Precipitation falls as rain, sleet, freezing rain, hail, and snow. When rain falls into a thick layer of air that is just above freezing and close to the ground, the raindrops turn into tiny ice pieces called sleet. Freezing rain occurs when rain falls through a layer of air close to the ground that is a little below freezing temperature. The rain freezes after it lands and coats everything in ice. Hail forms when ice crystals get pulled in a strong updraft repeatedly during a thunderstorm. Each time they rise, the ice pieces get larger. When they get heavy enough, they drop as hail. Hail can range in size from as small as a pea to as big as a grapefruit. Snow falls when falling ice crystals bump into each other and form snowflakes.

Run-off and Percolation

After precipitation, water "runs off" into streams, lakes, rivers, aquifers, and the seas. Run-off is minimal during drought or dry seasons. It increases during storms, rainy seasons, and when snow melts. The drainage area for a lake can stretch for hundreds of miles around it. Percolation is the process by which water slowly moves through the sand, soil, or rock until it reaches a body of water or an aquifer.

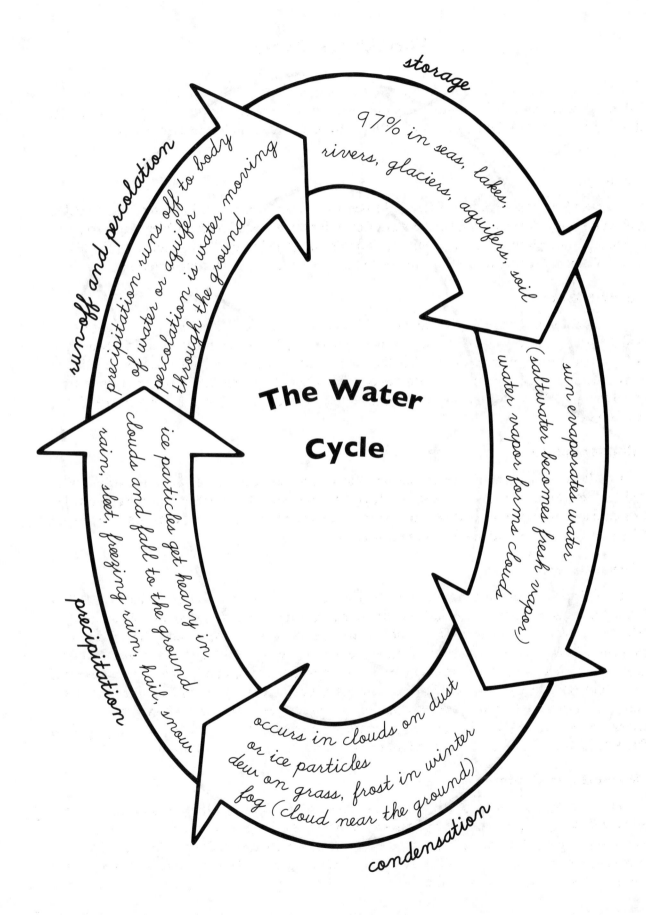

storage

97% in seas, lakes, rivers, glaciers, aquifers, soil

run-off and percolation

precipitation runs off to body of water or aquifer

percolation is water moving through the ground

sun evaporates water
(saltwater becomes fresh vapor;
water vapor forms clouds)

The Water Cycle

ice particles get heavy in clouds and fall to the ground

rain, sleet, freezing rain, hail, snow

precipitation

occurs in clouds on dust or ice particles

dew on grass, frost in winter

fog (cloud near the ground)

condensation

Science

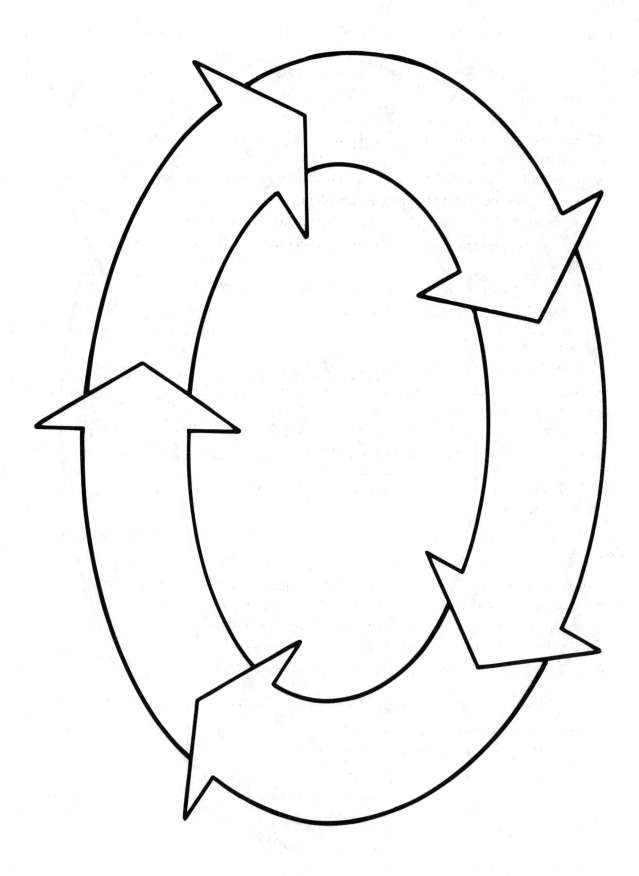

Day 1

1. Make student copies of "How Plants Reproduce" on pages 26–27. Introduce any unfamiliar vocabulary:
   - **pollen**—the fertilizing element of flowering plants, consisting of fine, powdery, yellowish grains
   - **germinate**—to put forth shoots; to sprout
   - **nutrients**—vitamins and minerals needed to sustain life
   - **liverwort**—a moss-like plant that grows chiefly on damp ground, rocks, or on tree trunks and helps to break down logs and even rocks
   - **horsetail**—a plant having a jointed hollow stem and narrow leaves
   - **vegetative**—pertaining to the plant kingdom
   - **rhizomes** (RYE-zomes)—plant stems that spread out underground

2. Distribute the copies and have the students read the article independently. It is written at a 4.6 reading level.

3. Make an overhead transparency and student copies of the Venn diagram on page 29.

4. As a class, discuss the passage. Show your students pictures of plant parts (from a science textbook or the Web). Point out that our fruit and vegetable crops would yield about 37 percent less without the assistance of insects (especially bees) in pollination. This means that wind alone is not an efficient method of pollination.

5. Distribute copies of the Venn diagram and display the overhead transparency. Fill in the graphic organizer as a class, using information from the passage. This is an ideal opportunity to help students determine how to distill a lengthy passage into its essential kernels of knowledge.

6. Help your students to understand that the intersection of the circles contains information relevant to both sexual and asexual reproduction. Include the names of the plants from the second page. Since all plants reproduce sexually and these are some of the ones that can do so asexually, they belong in the intersection.

Day 2

1. Distribute a blank copy of the "Venn Diagram" graphic organizer to each student.

2. Pair the students. Over the first circle, have them write "Flowering Plants." Over the right-hand circle, they should write "Coniferous Plants." Have the partners work together and refer to the "How Plants Reproduce" passage to fill in their Venn diagram.

3. Wipe the transparency clean and go over the answers with the class. Let them volunteer all of the

Flowering Plants	Coniferous Plants	Both
flowers, fruits, and vegetables insects & wind transfer pollen from one part of flower to other flowers turn into seeds after blooming some seeds fly to new spot animals eat fruit and pass seeds as waste fruit rots and provides nutrients to make seeds germinate	pines and spruces stay green year-round needles instead of leaves no flowers produce male (pollen) and female (ovule) cones wind transfers pollen between cones	have male and female parts pollination is necessary to start new plant some seeds germinate quickly some seeds take weeks, months, years, or an environmental event to germinate

Science

How Plants Reproduce

Plant Sexual Reproduction

Like all living organisms, plants reproduce. Most plants use sexual reproduction, which means that a male cell and a female cell must join to create a new plant. Flowering and coniferous plants sexually reproduce through seeds. Other plants sexually reproduce with spores.

Flowering Seeds

Flowering plants produce flowers that turn into seeds after blossoming. This includes all plants that produce fruits and vegetables. Flowers have a male part called a stamen and a female part called a pistil. A seed forms when the pollen from the stamen reaches the ovule (egg) in the pistil. Pollen can be moved by the wind, but often insects crawling around inside a flower spread it. Bees, butterflies, and beetles help the most with pollination.

Once an ovule is pollinated, it turns into a seed. Nutrients are inside the seed to give it the energy to germinate and make a tiny new sprout. The wind helps some seeds, such as those for dandelions and maple trees, soar through the air to a new spot. Other seeds develop a fruit covering. Moist, fleshy fruits include grapes, pumpkins, watermelons, and squash. Dry, hard fruits are things like peanuts, acorns, and pea pods. Fruit has two purposes. If an animal eats the fruit, it will pass the seeds as waste. Animal waste contains nutrients to help the seed start growing. If the fruit is not eaten, it falls to the ground and rots. Rotting breaks the fruit down into the nutrients that the seed needs.

Coniferous Seeds

Coniferous plants (pines, spruces, firs, etc.) do not have flowers. They have needles instead of leaves, stay green year-round, and produce cones. Conifers produce both male and female cones. The male cone has pollen. The female cone has an ovule (egg). Wind carries the pollen to the ovules, creating seeds. These seeds drop to the ground to start new pine trees.

Whether from a flowering or coniferous plant, some seeds germinate quickly. Others take weeks, months, or years to germinate. A few seeds will only germinate after the heat of a forest fire or when it rains in the desert after several years.

Spores

Plants such as mosses, liverworts, horsetails, and ferns reproduce with spores. Ferns make spores on the underside of their leaves. When the spores mature, they fall to the ground. Each tiny spore grows into a sprout. This sprout makes both sperm cells and an egg. When it rains, the sperm move to the egg and fertilize it. Then the sprout can grow into a new fern plant.

How Plants Reproduce *(cont.)*

Plant Asexual Reproduction

All plants reproduce sexually. Some plants can reproduce in other ways, too. For example, rose bushes can reproduce using seeds and roots. Asexual reproduction means that a new plant begins without a male cell and a female cell joining. This is also called vegetative reproduction, and it means that some plants start new plants through the use of their leaves, leaves, roots, runners, rhizomes, tubers, and bulbs.

Leaves

A few plants, such as the African violet or coleus, can start a new plant from their leaves. If a stem piece with a single leaf is soaked in water or pressed into damp soil, it will grow roots. When planted, it will become a whole new plant.

Roots

Some plants, like carrots and radishes, have roots that store food for the plant to use. Other plants send up new shoots from their roots. The shoots are called suckers and look like tiny plants as they emerge from the soil. These plants include raspberries and apple trees.

Runners and Rhizomes

Runners are stems that grow along the top of the ground and drop roots into the soil. More strawberry plants actually begin from runners than through seeds. Rhizomes (RYE-zomes) are stems that spread out underground. Grasses and many weeds grow from rhizomes.

Tubers and Bulbs

Some plants have underground stems that store food. They are called either tubers or bulbs. A potato is a tuber. It develops "eyes." These "eyes" are actually new roots. If the potato is not dug up, these roots will spread and start new plants.

Tulips, daffodils, lilies, and crocuses grow from bulbs. They re-grow each year from the same bulb. After blooming, these plants send all their remaining starch, or food, to the underground bulb. The next growing season those same bulbs grow roots, stems, leaves, and flowers. After blossoming, these plants "die down" and lie hidden underground in the bulb again. This cycle can go on for decades.

Plant Reproduction

Science

Asexual

- called vegetative reproduction
- start from existing plants' leaves, roots, runners, rhizomes, tubers (potato), or bulbs (tulip)

(overlap)
- new plants grow
- African violet
- coleus
- strawberry
- raspberry
- apple tree
- grass
- weeds
- roses
- potato
- tulip
- daffodil
- lily
- crocus

Sexual

- flowering and coniferous plants
- flowers have male and female parts
- male part is a stamen—it makes pollen
- female part is a pistil—it forms an ovule
- male pollen must touch female ovule to create seeds
- spores (ferns, mosses) grow into sprouts that have both male and female cells

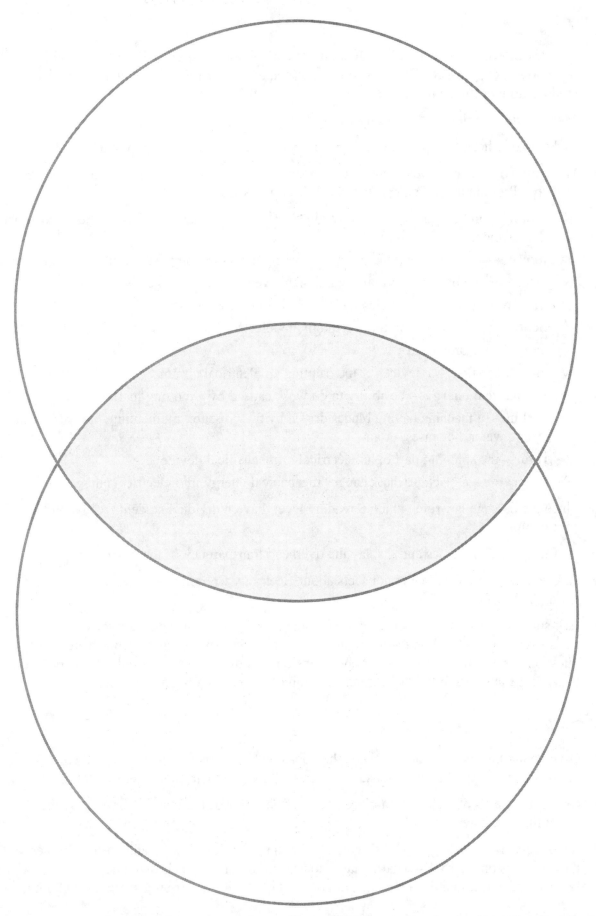

Science

Day 1

1. This lesson would be a good introduction to a unit about electricity. Before doing this lesson, have books, encyclopedias, access to the Internet, and other reference materials available for students to investigate this topic.

2. Make student copies of "Electricity Basics" on page 31.

3. Make an overhead transparency and student copies of the "K-W-L Chart" on page 33.

4. Write the vocabulary words below on the board. See if your students know the definition of any of them. Provide the definitions for any they do not know.

   ◇ **atom**—a tiny unit of matter; the smallest unit of an element that has all the characteristics of that element
   ◇ **nucleus**—the positively-charged center within an atom composed of neutrons and protons
   ◇ **electrons**—subatomic particles with a negative electrical charge
   ◇ **protons**—subatomic particles with a positive electrical charge
   ◇ **neutrons**—subatomic particles without any electrical charge
   ◇ **chaotic**—disorganized
   ◇ **circuit breaker**—a device for interrupting an electrical circuit
   ◇ **mechanical energy**—the ability to do work caused by a moving mass
   ◇ **turbine**—a machine having blades driven by the pressure, momentum, or thrust of moving steam, water, hot gases, or air
   ◇ **rotor**—the spinning part of an electrical or mechanical device
   ◇ **generator**—a machine that changes mechanical energy into electrical energy

5. Since the passage is written at a 6.8 reading level, have individual students read aloud each paragraph.

6. Distribute student copies and display the overhead transparency of the organizer.

7. Ask your students for three major facts about electricity from the passage. Use the information to fill in the "I Know" column.

8. Ask students what they wonder about electricity. Write three of their questions on the transparency in the "I Wonder" column. Each class member can choose to research those questions or questions of his or her choice (as long as three are researched). Explain that they are to write the answers in the "I Learned" column of the graphic organizer.

Days 2–3

1. Give your students time to investigate the books and other materials you've gathered. Depending on the complexity of the questions, you may need to give them time over several days.

2. Create a large K-W-L chart on a piece of poster board. List the questions posed by the class (from the transparency).

3. Reconvene as a whole group. Ask volunteers to provide the answers and write them across from the questions on the K-W-L chart. Have students who pursued their own questions offer what they learned and add it to the class chart. Keep the class K-W-L chart on display throughout the unit.

Electricity Basics

All of the matter we see around us is made of atoms. Each atom has electrons orbiting a nucleus of protons and neutrons. The electrons have a negative charge, and the protons have a positive charge. Neutrons have no charge. Just as with magnets, like charges repel and unlike charges attract. This means that the electrons are drawn to the protons. Electrons always flow from negatively-charged to positively-charged materials until the charges are balanced. As electrons move from one item to another, the imbalance between electrons and protons creates an electrical charge. This flow of electrons is called electrical current.

Conductors let electrons move through them in an efficient, organized way. Metals are the best conductors, especially copper, aluminum, silver, and gold. Poor conductors let electricity pass, but the electrons move in a chaotic way. They bump into each other and produce heat. Insulators actually block the flow of electrons. Things made of rubber, plastic, and glass are insulators.

In your home, it is usually copper wire that carries current. Appliances that produce heat, such as a hair dryer, an electric dryer, or an electric stove use copper wire to get the electricity from the outlet to the appliance. For the heating element, they use a poor conductor.

An electrical circuit is a path along which current flows. A circuit must be complete for the power to move through it. An on/off switch works because when it's turned on, the circuit is completed. When it's turned off, the circuit is disrupted. This stops the flow of electricity. Circuits can be wired in series or parallel. Series circuits are less common because they are troublesome. Consider a string of Christmas lights. If it's a series circuit, when one light goes out, they all quit. The electricity can't flow past the "weak link." Then you must find the bulb that burned out and replace it to get the string working again.

Parallel circuitry means that a break in one circuit won't affect the others. Household wiring is done this way. This lets multiple sources draw electricity at the same time from outlets. Inside a house, all the circuits start and end at the service panel, which has circuit breakers. Sometimes, when many things on the same circuit operate at once, a circuit demands too much power. Then the circuit breaker "trips." This stops electricity from flowing. Why? The wires could overheat and cause a fire. Power will not go to the outlets on that circuit until the circuit breaker is reset.

How is electrical power made at a power plant? Mechanical energy in the form of wind, falling water, or steam turns a turbine. The turbine turns a shaft, which turns a rotor inside a generator. The rotor has many large magnets set in a circle. As the rotor spins, these magnets push electrons through large copper wires positioned around the rotor. The faster the rotor turns, the more power it makes. Wires carry this power to homes and businesses. When you flip on a light switch, electricity travels 186,000 miles per second from the power plant to light the bulb.

K-W-L Chart

I Know	I Wonder	I Learned
Electricity is the movement of electrons.	What is static electricity and what causes it?	Static electricity happens when electrons jump from a negatively-charged item to a positively-charged one.
Metals are the best conductors.	What are transformers and why are they used?	Current leaves the power plant at a high voltage to help it to travel long distance, but homes and businesses need lower voltage. Transformers can increase or decrease voltage as needed. They are inside boxes on the ground (for underground wires) or on poles (for overland wires).
Poor conductors let electricity move but cause heat.	What is a kilowatt and how many does the average family use in one year?	A kilowatt is equal to 1,000 watts per hour. It equals the amount of electricity used to light a 40-watt bulb for 25 hours. The average U.S. home uses 8,000 kilowatts each year.

Science

K-W-L Chart

I Know

I Wonder

I Learned

Day 1

1. This lesson is a good introduction to the history of Ancient Egypt.

2. Make student copies of the completed "Ancient Egyptian History: First Five Periods" on page 36. Introduce any unfamiliar vocabulary:

   ✧ **domesticated**—tamed and raised

   ✧ **centralized**—brought under the control of one

   ✧ **divine**—godlike, like or of a supreme being

   ✧ **prosperous**—wealthy, rich, successful

   ✧ **papyrus scrolls**—a material on which to write that is prepared from thin strips of the pith of the papyrus plant laid together, soaked, pressed, and dried

   ✧ **famine**—a lack of food in an area over a period of time

   ✧ **upheaval**—a sudden, violent disruption

   ✧ **nobles**—persons having a high social rank

   ✧ **diagnostic**—identifying a disease, problem, etc., based upon its symptoms

   ✧ **annex**—to add territory to a larger territory

3. Explain that Ancient Egyptian history is separated into 10 periods based on changes in Egyptian power, rulers, and lifestyle. Since this all happened thousands of years ago, it is hard to have exact dates, so many of the dates are approximations. The times given in this lesson come from research done by the Royal Ontario Museum in Toronto, Canada. All the years shown are B.C.E. (which stands for "Before the Current Era"). B.C.E. dates are counted back from the year 1 C.E., which is the approximate year of Jesus of Nazareth's birth. There is no year 0. C.E. stands for "The Current Era." Thus, the year 5500 B.C.E. is 2,400 years prior to 3100 B.C.E. You will need to explain this system to your students, who are used to a larger number meaning a later date.

4. Distribute student copies of the completed "Ancient Egyptian History: First Five Periods." Discuss each part of the graphic organizer.

Days 2–3

1. Have access to the Internet, books on ancient Egypt, and encyclopedias available for student use.

2. Make student copies of the "Facts About Ancient Egypt" on page 35 and the "Pyramid Time Line" graphic organizer on page 38.

3. Form groups of three. Distribute the student copies of pages 35 and 38. The students must do research to determine where each event is located on the time line.

4. Each student should submit a neatly prepared "Pyramid Time Line" to you. The answer key is provided on page 37. You may want to make an overhead transparency of it and go over it with the class after you've had a chance to check your students' work.

Directions: Title your pyramid time line "Ancient Egyptian History: Second Five Periods." Then write the dates given on the left-hand side of the "Pyramid Time Line" and the time period on the right-hand side. Do research to determine during which period each event below occurred. The number of facts given for each time period are noted in the chart. The facts with dates are the easiest to place, so place those first.

Time Period	Dates	Facts Given
Second Intermediate	1674–1567 B.C.E.	2 facts
New Kingdom	1567–1085 B.C.E.	4 facts
Third Intermediate	1085–715 B.C.E.	2 facts
Late Dynastic	715–332 B.C.E.	3 facts
Greco-Roman	332–30 B.C.E.	3 facts

- Cleopatra VII reigns from 51–30 B.C.E.
- internal fighting allows Nubians to conquer Egypt
- Hyksos kings take control of lower Egypt
- female pharaoh Hatshepsut rules
- pharaoh holds some power at Thebes
- warrior pharaohs regain control and annex other areas
- Greek warrior Alexander the Great takes over Egypt
- Roman Empire annexes Egypt in 30 B.C.E.
- Egypt reaches the height of its power and wealth
- Assyrians conquer Egypt; then Persians conquer Egypt in 525 B.C.E.
- Egypt is no longer a world power
- Egyptians regain power in 404 B.C.E.
- Persian King Darius builds a canal from the Nile to the Red Sea
- tribute from conquered peoples makes Egypt rich

Ancient Egyptian History: First Five Periods

History

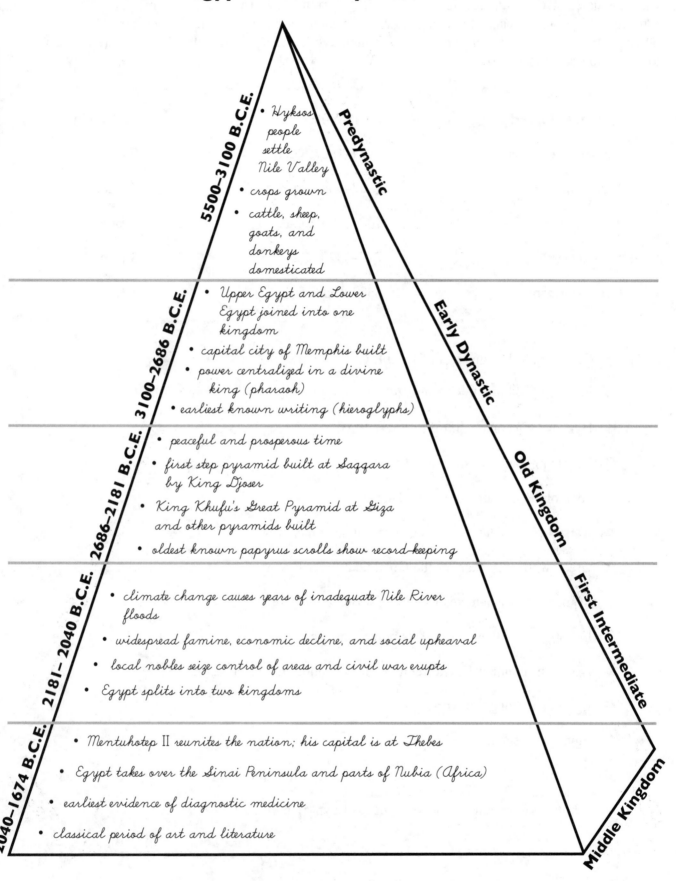

5500–3100 B.C.E. — **Predynastic**
- Hyksos people settle Nile Valley
- crops grown
- cattle, sheep, goats, and donkeys domesticated

3100–2686 B.C.E. — **Early Dynastic**
- Upper Egypt and Lower Egypt joined into one kingdom
- capital city of Memphis built
- power centralized in a divine king (pharaoh)
- earliest known writing (hieroglyphs)

2686–2181 B.C.E. — **Old Kingdom**
- peaceful and prosperous time
- first step pyramid built at Saqqara by King Djoser
- King Khufu's Great Pyramid at Giza and other pyramids built
- oldest known papyrus scrolls show record-keeping

2181– 2040 B.C.E. — **First Intermediate**
- climate change causes years of inadequate Nile River floods
- widespread famine, economic decline, and social upheaval
- local nobles seize control of areas and civil war erupts
- Egypt splits into two kingdoms

2040–1674 B.C.E. — **Middle Kingdom**
- Mentuhotep II reunites the nation; his capital is at Thebes
- Egypt takes over the Sinai Peninsula and parts of Nubia (Africa)
- earliest evidence of diagnostic medicine
- classical period of art and literature

Ancient Egyptian History: Second Five Periods

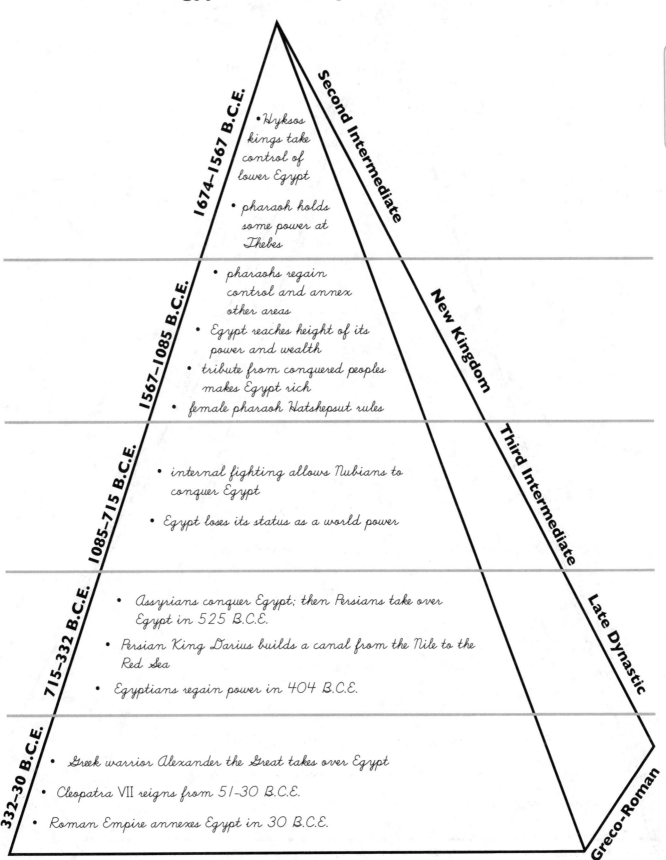

1674–1567 B.C.E.
- Hyksos kings take control of lower Egypt
- pharaoh holds some power at Thebes

Second Intermediate

1567–1085 B.C.E.
- pharaohs regain control and annex other areas
- Egypt reaches height of its power and wealth
- tribute from conquered peoples makes Egypt rich
- female pharaoh Hatshepsut rules

New Kingdom

1085–715 B.C.E.
- internal fighting allows Nubians to conquer Egypt
- Egypt loses its status as a world power

Third Intermediate

715–332 B.C.E.
- Assyrians conquer Egypt; then Persians take over Egypt in 525 B.C.E.
- Persian King Darius builds a canal from the Nile to the Red Sea
- Egyptians regain power in 404 B.C.E.

Late Dynastic

332–30 B.C.E.
- Greek warrior Alexander the Great takes over Egypt
- Cleopatra VII reigns from 51–30 B.C.E.
- Roman Empire annexes Egypt in 30 B.C.E.

Greco-Roman

History

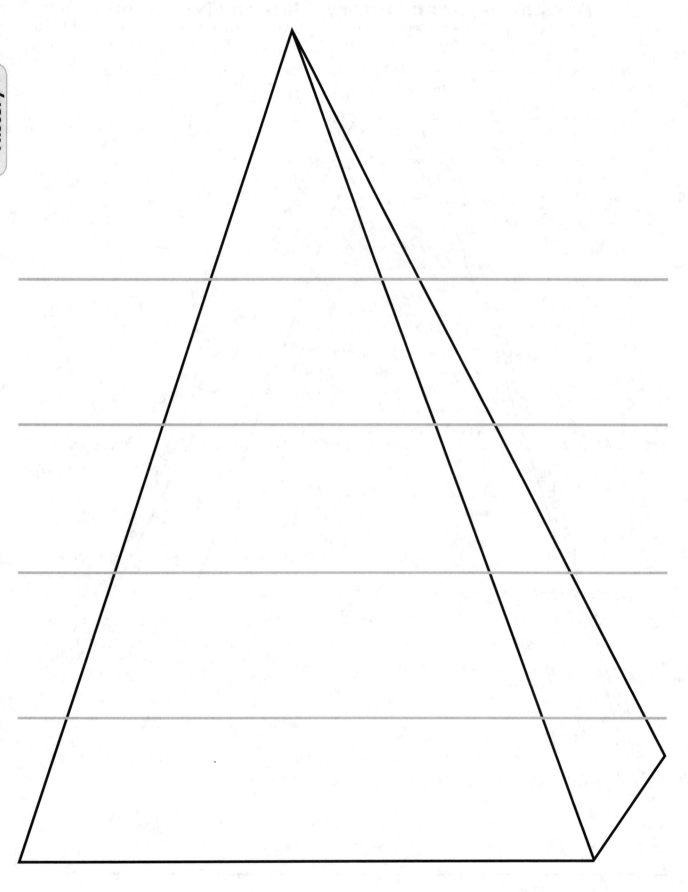

1. Discuss what a myth is (*a legend, usually concerning some hero or event, especially one that is concerned with gods and explains some practice, rite, or phenomenon of nature*) and why ancient peoples created them (*to explain nature; to solidify collective beliefs; to justify social institutions*).

2. Make copies of the myth "The Founding of Rome: The Story of Romulus and Remus" on page 40.

3. Make an overhead transparency and copies of the "Literature Guide" graphic organizer on page 42.

4. Show your students where Rome is on a world map. Discuss why a great city would have been built in this location (*mild climate good for growing crops; near the Mediterranean Sea, so they could trade with other civilizations using ships; etc.*).

5. Introduce any unfamiliar vocabulary:

   ✧ **paranoid**—unjustified suspicions and mistrust about others

   ✧ **immortal**—living forever

   ✧ **devouring**—eating, consuming

   ✧ **imprisoned**—kept in jail or locked up

   ✧ **elder**—older

   ✧ **solitary**—spending time alone

   ✧ **thereafter**—afterward; from then on

   ✧ **dwell**—live

6. Distribute student copies of "The Founding of Rome: The Story of Romulus and Remus." It is written at a 6.3 reading level, so depending upon the needs of your class, read it as a whole group, as partners, or independently.

7. Display the overhead of the "Literature Guide." Discuss and fill in each part. For the title, setting, and characters, refer to the myth.

8. Explain that a theme is the underlying idea in a piece of literature. Determining the theme will give students exercise in inferential skills since it is not stated within the myth. Ask questions to guide the class to identify the theme of leadership.

9. Ask your students to name the five major events. This requires synthesis skills. Since there are more than five events in the story, students will probably give you more than the five you want. List all their responses on the board or a blank transparency, and then ask questions to guide the class to identify the five most major events by asking, "Which of all the events were the most important?" Condense the information and write it on the graphic organizer.

10. The most crucial information on the graphic organizer comes last. Stories such as the Romulus and Remus myth strongly influenced the people of ancient Rome by reinforcing the values of their culture. What are the values and beliefs taught by this myth? Your students must distill the information in the story into five values and beliefs. Since this also requires synthesis skills, it may be somewhat challenging.

Note: The "Literature Guide" graphic organizer can be used with any fiction piece.

History

The Founding of Rome:
The Story of Romulus and Remus

In the beginning, Amulius was the ruler of Alba Longa, a city on the banks of the River Tiber. He was a cruel and paranoid man. He feared that his nephews, the sons of his brother Numitor, would try to take control. The evil Amulius had Numitor's sons killed and his daughter, Rhea Silvia, held prisoner. This made the great god Mars furious with Amulius. Mars loved Rhea Silvia. She had given birth to his twin sons.

Wicked Amulius had Rhea Silvia and her newborn twins thrown into the River Tiber, but Mars watched over them. The river god Tiberinus saved Rhea Silvia and made her his immortal wife. Mars made the current quickly bring the twins to shore. Then he led his favorite animal, a she-wolf, to them. Instead of devouring the cold and hungry babies, she brought each one back to her den and nursed them with her own cubs. As his sons grew, Mars commanded flocks of birds to bring them bread and wild fruit each day.

Near the wolf's den lived Faustolo and his wife Laurentia. They were poor but good-hearted folk. One day Faustolo found the toddlers playing near the wolf's den. Since it was in the wilderness and he saw no other people about, he thought that they had been abandoned. He picked up a boy under each arm and carried them home. Faustolo named them Romulus and Remus. The boys viewed the couple as their parents.

When Romulus and Remus grew to be men, they learned their life story and returned to Alba Longa. There they killed the cruel Amulius, who had imprisoned their grandfather, Numitor. Soon after they freed him, Numitor became king of Alba Longa.

In April of 753 B.C.E., Romulus and Remus returned to the area along the River Tiber where they had grown up. They decided to start their own kingdom, but they could not decide who would be the ruler. As twins, neither one was the elder. So Remus went to Aventine Hill and Romulus went to Palatine Hill to await a sign from the gods. First Remus saw six vultures flying together. These usually solitary birds are sacred to the gods. Seeing so many together was surely a sign. Shortly thereafter, however, Romulus saw 12 vultures soaring in the sky.

When the men returned, they argued over which was more important: Remus seeing the sign first or Romulus seeing the greater number of birds. Since no one could say for certain, Romulus decided to take action. He took a plow and made furrows to mark the city's perimeter. Then he began building a wall. Remus climbed over the wall and laughingly said, "This won't protect you, and it proves nothing!" That made Romulus so angry that he killed Remus with a sword. Then Romulus became king and named the city Rome in his own honor. Romulus ruled wisely until one stormy day when he was carried off by Mars to live forever in the place where the gods dwell.

Title _The Founding of Rome: The Story of Romulus and Remus_

History

Setting

> **When?** around 758 B.C.E. (about 2,700–2,800 years ago)
>
> **Where?** Mediterranean Basin/Rome (present day Italy)

Main Characters   Amulius   Numitor   Mars

                                       Rhea Silvia   Romulus   Remus

Theme

> The theme is leadership and power: choosing a leader, staying a leader, and behavior as a leader.

Major Event 1   Evil King Amulius has Numitor's sons killed and his daughter imprisoned.

Major Event 2   Mars has Rhea Silvia give birth to twin sons.

Major Event 3   Although Amulius tries to kill Rhea Silvia and her sons, the boys are raised by a wolf.

Major Event 4   When grown, Romulus and Remus kill Amulius and free their grandfather.

Major Event 5   After Romulus and Remus argue, Romulus kills Remus and becomes Rome's first ruler.

What values and beliefs were taught in this story?

Wickedness will be punished.

A wise, strong leader is desirable; an evil one is terrible.

Violence is often necessary to establish leadership.

The gods take an active role in people's lives and fate.

The gods send signs, although they aren't always clear.

History

Title _____

Setting
┌───┐
│ *When?*   │
│   │
│ *Where?*   │
└───┘

Main Characters   _____   _____   _____

                       _____   _____   _____

Theme
┌───┐
│   │
│   │
└───┘

Major Event 1 _____

_____

Major Event 2 _____

Major Event 3 _____

_____

Major Event 4 _____

_____

Major Event 5 _____

_____

What values and beliefs were taught in this story?

_____

_____

_____

_____

_____

_____

1. Tell your students that you are going to ask them some questions to guide their thinking, but they are not to say the answers. Then say, "Think about a time when you were really sick. What were your symptoms? How did you feel? Were you afraid that you would not get better? How did the members of your family act while you were sick? Did people avoid you?"

2. Explain that a horrible disease struck during the Middle Ages that changed the course of history and made everyday life challenging for the people in Asia, Europe, and Africa. This is a disease unlike any your students have ever experienced.

3. Distribute copies of "The Black Death Devastates Asia and Europe" on page 44 and have your students read the article. It is written at a 5.4 reading level. Introduce any unfamiliar vocabulary:

   ✧ **devastate**—destroy, overwhelm

   ✧ **pandemic**—an epidemic (serious illness) spread over a large geographic area and affecting a huge number of the population

   ✧ **bubonic plague**—an often fatal disease spread by bacteria

   ✧ **associated**—in a relationship with, allied

   ✧ **perished**—died

   ✧ **resistance**—the ability to oppose or resist

   ✧ **immunity**—the condition that lets a person be insusceptible to a particular disease

   ✧ **susceptible**—able to be affected

   ✧ **humanity**—all humans collectively; the human race; humankind

   ✧ **antibiotics**—drugs that kill or stop the growth of microorganisms (bacteria)

4. Make an overhead transparency of the completed "Question-Answer Relationships" graphic organizer on page 45. Make one copy of the blank graphic organizer on page 46.

5. Write the questions in the first column of the completed "Question-Answer Relationships" graphic organizer on the blank graphic organizer. Then make student copies of this graphic organizer.

6. Explain that the questions typically asked by textbooks, teachers, and tests have one of three types of answers:

   • **Stated (S)**—The answer is easy to find because the words used in the questions and the words in the text are identical.

   • **Look for it (L)**—The words used in the passage and the words in the question are different but similar.

   • **Think about it (T)**—The answer is not in the text. Finding it requires students to combine the text information with what they know to frame a response.

7. Distribute the copies of the organizer. Display the overhead transparency, keeping each row covered by a strip of paper. As a class, read a question, then decide on its coding and the answer. The answers must be written in complete sentences. Show students how to take words from the question to formulate the answers. Remove the strip of paper so that the students can see just that row. Do the entire graphic organizer together.

Extension: Write more questions based on the passage on another copy of the graphic organizer and then make student copies. Have the students complete the graphic organizers as homework.

History

The Black Death
Devastates Europe and Asia

Historians believe that the world's worst pandemic was the bubonic plague. Also called the Black Death, it first struck in southwestern China. Ships carried infected rats from there to the Mediterranean Sea. Once the rats reached shore, they scurried across Europe, leaving a path of terror and death. This disease killed between one-third and one-half of Europe's whole population. It began in the late 1340s and lasted more than 350 years.

Back then people knew nothing about germs. They had no idea how disease spread. Although they made soap, they did not understand the importance of cleanliness and lived in filthy conditions. Now we know that fleas carried the bubonic plague bacteria. These fleas bit the rats that lived in people's homes. It was common for people to be bitten by both rats and fleas, but nobody realized that such a bite was a death sentence. To make matters worse, just before the bubonic plague broke out, Europeans had killed cats because they thought that cats were associated with the devil. Fewer cats meant more rats, and each rat harbored the plague-infested fleas in its fur.

People called the plague the Black Death because the victim's skin turned black. It started out with red rings on the skin followed by a high fever and coughing up blood. A person also might develop painful swellings. Nearly 75 percent of those who caught it died. In Paris alone, more than 50,000 people perished. Most died within three days; some died in a day. When patients coughed, the germs spread through the air. Once a person fell ill, his or her house was sealed for 40 days. A cross was painted on the door to warn others. No one could go in or out.

There were no funerals because people would not gather for a ceremony. They never knew who would fall ill next. So each day carts moved through the streets. The driver would cry, "Bring out your dead!" Doors opened. People carried their dead loved ones to the wagon and threw them in. So many people were dying so fast that there wasn't the time or materials to make caskets. The corpses were stacked in mass graves. Entire families perished. Some people were so terrified that they abandoned a family member at the first sign of illness. Many of those who fled to the countryside brought the disease with them. Nowhere was safe.

By 1698, the disease had claimed 25 million victims in Europe. At least another 50 million died in Asia and Africa. No wonder many people thought that no one would survive and the world would end! But those who did survive seemed to develop resistance to the disease. Since they were the only people left to reproduce, they passed on this immunity to their offspring. Slowly the bubonic plague ran out of susceptible victims.

Could the bubonic plague devastate humanity again? No one knows for sure. The bacteria still exists. But now we have antibiotics that can kill it.

Code each question with one of these letters:

S = the answer was **stated** in the text

L = you had to **look** for the answer in the text

T = you had to **think** about it to come up with the answer; it was not given in the text

Question	Code	Answer
1. Where did the Black Death begin?	L	The Black Death began in southwestern China and traveled to Europe via rats on ships.
2. Why did people call the bubonic plague the Black Death?	S	People called the plague the Black Death because the victims' skin turned black.
3. What were the symptoms of the bubonic plague?	L	The symptoms included red rings on the skin, high fever, coughing up blood, painful swellings, and blackened skin.
4. Approximately how many people died worldwide from the bubonic plague?	T	A total of at least 75 million people died (25 million in Europe and 50 million in Africa and Asia).
5. Could the Black Death devastate humanity again?	T	We now have antibiotics to fight the disease, but if it happened in an undeveloped nation, many might die before the antibiotics reached the area.

History

Code each question with one of these letters:

S = the answer was **stated** in the text

L = you had to **look** for the answer in the text

T = you had to **think** about it to come up with the answer; it was not given in the text

	Question	Code	Answer
1.			
2.			
3.			
4.			
5.			

Day 1

1. Using an anticipation guide piques your students' curiosity and encourages them to read actively to locate answers. Make one copy of the "Anticipation Guide" graphic organizer on page 50. On the first line, write the topic "Buddhism." Then write these five statements next to the numbers on the graphic organizer:

   • Buddha was a human being who lived and died long ago.

   • Buddhism began in China and spread around the world.

   • Today, Buddhism is the world religion with the largest number of believers.

   • Buddhists believe that by giving up all worldly desires and attachments to this world, one can get beyond suffering and the cycle of birth and death.

   • There has already been one Buddha and another will come in the future.

2. Now make student copies of this "Anticipation Guide" and distribute them.

3. Ask the students to independently read each statement and label it true or false.

4. Make student copies of "Major World Religions: Buddhism" on page 48. It is written at a 6.9 reading level, so read this passage aloud to the class as they follow along.

5. After the reading is done, have your students fix any statements they marked wrong by crossing out the word "True" or "False" and writing the correct answer.

6. Collect the graphic organizers to check for understanding. The correct responses are shown on the completed graphic organizer on page 49. You may want to make an overhead transparency of that page to use during the next day's discussion.

Day 2

1. Return the "Anticipation Guides" and discuss the correct answers.

2. Make an overhead transparency and student copies of the "Knowledge Tier" organizer on page 52.

3. Explain to your students that today there is an overabundance of information available. They cannot possibly remember everything that they read. Thus, when they read, they need to distinguish between facts that they should remember (essential information), facts that are interesting (useful information), and facts that will be probably be forgotten (expert information). This requires advanced thinking skills, so your students will need direct instruction to learn how to do it.

4. Display the "Knowledge Tier" transparency and distribute the student copies.

5. Have students take out their copies of "Major World Religions: Buddhism."

6. Go through the passage and determine the tiers in which the facts belong. It's critical for you and the students to discuss each decision. Answers are shown in the completed graphic organizer on page 51. For the base tier, choose the three most important concepts that the students should remember and build. This is core knowledge that all literate adults know. For the middle tier, choose three concepts that will be useful knowledge—things that may be forgotten after the unit but that the student may be able to remember later in response to a stimulus. At the top, put three details that will probably be forgotten. These are things most literate adults do not know, although they probably can locate the information.

History

Major World Religions: Buddhism

Buddha Shakyamuni was born Prince Siddhartha Gautama (sih-DAR-tuh GOW-tuh-muh) in 563 BC in India. He grew up in a palace and married a princess. At the age of 29, he had visions. He saw an old man, an ill man, a dead man, and a holy man. From the first three visions he learned that life always includes aging, illness, and death. The vision of the holy man made Gautama decide to leave his wife and son to seek truth. So he gave up his family, wealth, and status and spent six years on this quest.

One day he meditated under a tree. After many hours in a trance, he achieved enlightenment and became the Buddha (the Enlightened One). From that day on, Buddha preached the *dharma* (saving truth). One of the most sacred events in Buddhism was his first sermon. He spoke it to five men near the city of Varanasi. He said that life was a continuous cycle of death and rebirth. Each time a person was born, his status was determined by his actions in his prior life. The only escape from this cycle of rebirth was through moral purity, which could be attained by following the Noble Eightfold Path of

- knowing the truth
- choosing to resist evil
- saying nothing to hurt others
- respecting life, morality, and property

- doing a job that does not hurt others
- striving to free one's mind of evil
- controlling one's feelings and thoughts
- practicing proper concentration.

Buddha told people to chant *sutras* to achieve a better reincarnation. The Diamond Sutra is one such sacred work and is the earliest known printed book. Created by woodblock print in 868 C.E., it tells of the Buddha's belief that humans must seek the true and timeless reality beyond our visible world. He insisted that the absence of all desire was necessary for happiness. Only overcoming the longing for worldly things could lead a person to *nirvana*, a state of true joy.

Buddha preached the dharma in India. Over time, Buddha organized his followers into groups of monks and nuns. He died at about the age of 80.

Sometime between 100 and 200 C.E., traders brought the Buddhist message to China. Its popularity spread among the peasants there. They had thought that heaven was for kings and hell for all other people. The idea that a person's actions could affect his or her afterlife or reincarnation was thrilling. Many Chinese sculptures are based on Buddhism. Today, most Buddhists live in Southeast Asia, Japan, and parts of Russia. About six percent of the world's population practice Buddhism.

Miroku Bosatsu is the Buddha of the Future. He will appear 5.6 billion years after Buddha's death. Before he arrives, the teachings of the first Buddha will be forgotten. The new Buddha is supposed to achieve perfect enlightenment, preach the true Dharma, and unite the world.

> **Note:** This has been filled in based on how the majority of your students probably responded to the statements.

Before you read about ___*Buddhism*___ , look at these sentences. Based on what you know about the topic, write "True" on the line if you think that the statement is true. Write "False" on the line if you think that the statement is false.

___*True*___ **1. Buddha was a human who lived and died long ago.**

___*True*___ **2. Buddhism began in China and spread around the world.**

Buddhism began in India and spread to China hundreds of years later. Over time it spread around the world.

___*True*___ **3. Today, Buddhism is the world religion with the largest number of believers.**

Just six percent of the world's population is Buddhist.

___*True*___ **4. Buddhists believe that by giving up all worldly desires, one can achieve true and lasting happiness.**

___*False*___ **5. There has already been one Buddha, and another will come in the future.**

The first Buddha lived about 1,400 years ago. Another Buddha will come 5.6 billion years after the first one's death.

History

Before you read about _____ , look at these sentences. Based on what you know about the topic, write "True" on the line if you think that the statement is true. Write "False" on the line if you think that the statement is false.

_____ **1.**

_____ **2.**

_____ **3.**

_____ **4.**

_____ **5.**

History

Buddha Shakyamuni was born
Prince Siddhartha Gautama.

Miroku Bosatsu is the Buddha
of the Future.

Buddhists chant sutras to achieve
a better reincarnation.

**Expert
Knowledge**

Buddha lived about 1,400 years ago.

Another Buddha will appear in the distant
future.

Buddhists believe that when a person stops
wanting things, he can reach nirvana
(a state of true joy).

**Useful
Knowledge**

Buddha was a human who became enlightened (knew the truth).

Buddhists believe in reincarnation. Each time a person is born,
his status is determined by his actions in his prior life.

Buddhism began in India and spread into China and
Southeast Asia.

Essential Knowledge

History

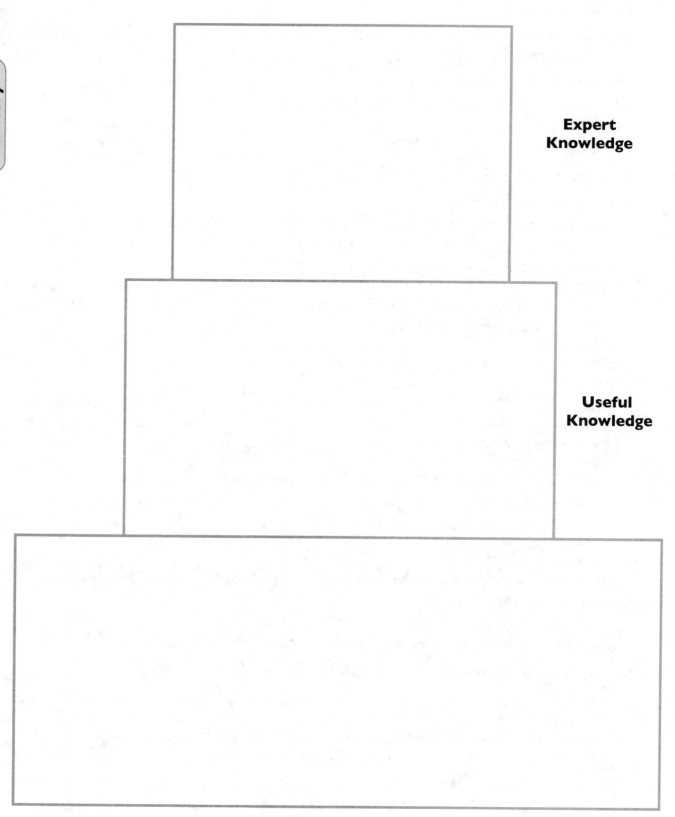

**Expert
Knowledge**

**Useful
Knowledge**

Essential Knowledge

1. Display a world map.

2. Make student copies of the poem "The Months" on page 54. Introduce any unfamiliar vocabulary:
   - **desolate**—barren, lonely
   - **ranges**—passes through
   - **scorched**—dried out and withered by intense heat
   - **disrobe**—undress
   - **keen**—sharp, biting

3. Distribute the student copies and read the poem chorally.

4. Use these questions for discussion:
   - Does this poem accurately portray the weather that occurs in your area during each month? Why or why not?
   - What are Earth's four hemispheres? (*Eastern, Western, Northern, and Southern*) How are they divided? (*The Eastern and Western are split at the prime meridian (0° longitude); the Northern and Southern are split at the equator (0° latitude).*) Have students point out these answers on the world map.
   - In what areas on Earth would this poem be applicable? (*It would be applicable for much of the temperate zone in the Northern Hemisphere.*)
   - In what areas on Earth would this poem not be applicable? (*This poem would not be applicable to places in the Southern Hemisphere, since their seasons are the exact opposite of the ones in the Northern Hemisphere due to the Earth's tilt. Also, the poem wouldn't apply to the tropics where the seasons are almost indistinguishable since the amount of sunlight and temperatures vary little throughout the year.*)
   - Would this poem apply to people living in the Eastern and Western Hemispheres? (*Yes, if they are also in the Northern Hemisphere; no, if they are also in the Southern Hemisphere.*) Have student volunteers give examples of each.
   - Why do different regions of the Northern Hemisphere have such different climates? (*Each has seasons based on how close it lies to the equator, Tropic of Cancer (23°27'N), and Arctic Circle (66°33'N).*) Have your students come up and point out these three lines of latitude on the world map.
   - Why do different regions of the Southern Hemisphere have such different climates? (*Climate is based on how close the area lies to the equator, Tropic of Capricorn (23°27'S), and Antarctic Circle (66°33'S).*) Have your students come up and point out these three lines of latitude on the world map.
   - What is the region between the Tropic of Cancer and the Tropic of Capricorn called? What is it like? (*It's called the tropics. The climate in the tropics does not have clearly defined seasons like those in the "temperate zones," which lie between the tropics and the Arctic Circle or Antarctic Circle. The temperature and weather vary little throughout the year.*)

5. Make an overhead transparency and two copies for each student of the "Mayan Step Pyramid" organizer on page 56. Display the transparency and distribute one of the student copies.

6. Keep the world map visible. As a class, fill in the graphic organizer for the tropics.

7. Pair the students. Distribute the second copy of the graphic organizer and have the students complete it for hemispheres.

Geography

The Months
by Christina Rossetti

January cold and desolate;

February dripping wet;

March wind ranges;

April changes;

Birds sing in tune

To flowers of May,

And sunny June

Brings longest day;

In scorched July

The storm clouds fly,

Lightning-torn;

August bears corn,

September fruit;

In rough October

Earth must disrobe her;

Stars fall and shoot

In keen November;

And night is long

And cold is strong

In bleak December.

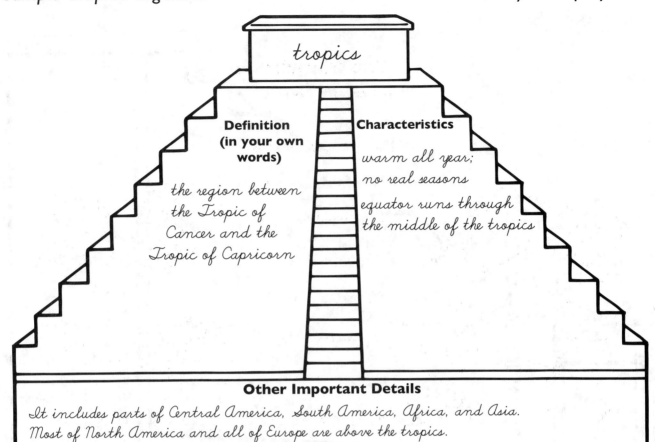

tropics

Definition (in your own words)

the region between the Tropic of Cancer and the Tropic of Capricorn

Characteristics

warm all year; no real seasons

equator runs through the middle of the tropics

Other Important Details

It includes parts of Central America, South America, Africa, and Asia.
Most of North America and all of Europe are above the tropics.
Australia and Antarctica are below the tropics.

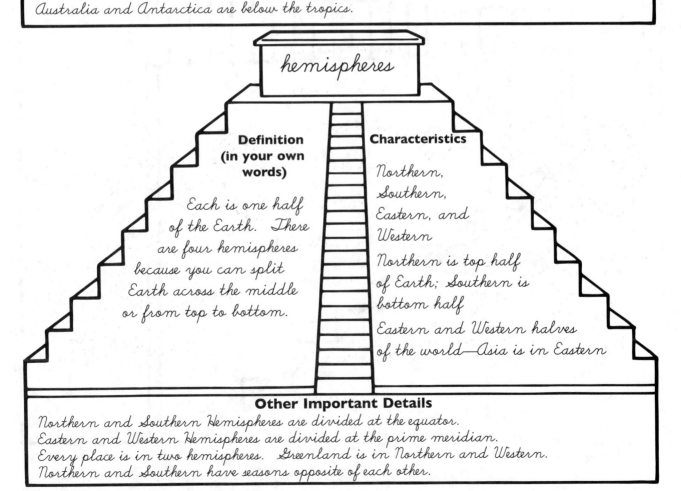

hemispheres

Definition (in your own words)

Each is one half of the Earth. There are four hemispheres because you can split Earth across the middle or from top to bottom.

Characteristics

Northern, Southern, Eastern, and Western

Northern is top half of Earth; Southern is bottom half

Eastern and Western halves of the world—Asia is in Eastern

Other Important Details

Northern and Southern Hemispheres are divided at the equator.
Eastern and Western Hemispheres are divided at the prime meridian.
Every place is in two hemispheres. Greenland is in Northern and Western.
Northern and Southern have seasons opposite of each other.

Geography

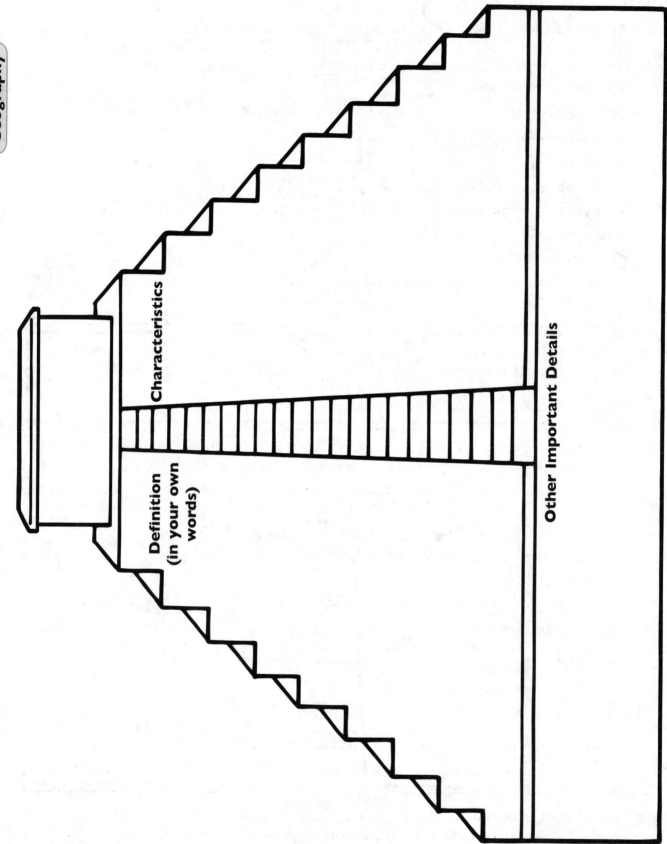

Characteristics

Definition (in your own words)

Other Important Details

Day 1

1. This lesson should be taught after your students know the characteristics of ecosystems, and preferably after they have studied at least one ecosystem in depth. This lesson shows that documented disasters and the affected ecosystems' recoveries have proven ecosystems' surprising resilience.

2. Make student copies of "Ecosystems Bounce Back" on page 58. Introduce vocabulary:

   ✧ **catastrophes**—disasters
   ✧ **inhabit**—live in
   ✧ **devastated**—destroyed
   ✧ **habitat**— the natural environment of an organism; where it is typically found
   ✧ **germinate**—start to grow
   ✧ **charred**—burned
   ✧ **phosphate**—a salt of phosphoric acid used in fertilizer (and at one time, laundry soaps) that can cause algae overgrowth if it gets into a water source
   ✧ **atmospheric**—involving the layers of air above Earth's surface

3. Distribute the student copies. This passage is written at a 6.5 reading level. Based on the needs of your class, you can have your students read it independently, in pairs, or as a whole group.

4. Questions for discussion after reading:

   • Which ecosystem's recovery was the most amazing? Why do you think so?
   • Why does it take decades for an area destroyed by a volcano to recover? (*Wind and water erosion and the decay of spiders are slow processes needed to create soil.*)
   • Why do forests and neighboring meadows recover so rapidly from a major blaze? (*Forests depend on blazes to release nutrients. Some trees can't even germinate without a fire.*)
   • What is causing global warming? (*greenhouse gases caused by burning fossil fuels*)
   • What can we do to stop global warming? (*reduce amount of fossil fuel burned—use other energy sources*)

5. Make an overhead transparency and student copies of the "Chain of Events" organizer on page 60.

6. Display the transparency and distribute the student copies. As a class, fill in the six major events discussed in the paragraph about ecosystems recovering from a volcano. The answers are shown on the completed graphic organizer on page 59.

Day 2

1. Distribute fresh student copies of the "Chain of Events" graphic organizer.

2. Pair your students and have them discuss and then fill in the six major events for the paragraphs about ecosystems recovering from forest fires. Collect the graphic organizers and check them.

3. Distribute a fresh copy of the "Chain of Events" graphic organizer. For homework, have your students independently complete it using the paragraph about Lake Erie. Be sure to collect this graphic organizer to check for understanding.

Geography

Ecosystems Bounce Back

Sometimes events happen in an ecosystem that would seem to destroy it forever. But nature has a way of recovering from catastrophes—although it does so gradually. For example, after a volcanic eruption, everything lies buried under lava, ashes, or mud. It looks as if life will never again inhabit the area. But that's not the case. Spiders blown in by the wind bring life back to volcano-devastated regions. As the dead spiders decay, they leave the elements essential to all life: nitrogen, carbon, and oxygen. Wind and water erosion breaks down the hardened lava. It turns into soil. This process may take decades. Eventually there is enough dirt for wind-borne seeds to take root and grow.

A forest fire is another event that appears to destroy an ecosystem. Yet forests need fires to release the minerals stored in dead and living plants and trees. A fire keeps the forest from taking over the meadows that border it. After a large fire, these fields grow fast due to the nutrients set free by the blaze. So, forest fires make new habitats. This promotes greater plant and animal variety. The highest number of different species is found about 25 years after a major blaze.

In 1988 Yellowstone National Park had a forest fire that lasted three months. The gigantic blaze burned about a million acres. But just one year later, the forest showed new growth. Its most plentiful trees are lodge pole pines. They have cones that need the high temperature of a fire to open and drop their seeds. These cones lay on the ground for years waiting for a fire to let them germinate. Their tiny saplings poked up through the charred soil, and a flowering plant called fireweed blanketed the area.

Even a dead lake can come back to life. By the late 1960s, so much pollution had been dumped into Lake Erie that most of its fish had died. Thick mats of green slime floated on its surface, and the lake's whole ecosystem broke down. In 1972 the Canadian and American governments agreed to clean up the lake. But scientists had declared the lake dead. No one knew if it could be saved. The most damaging pollutant was the phosphate in laundry soap. So soap makers removed the chemical. New laws required all waste be treated before entering the lake. After 10 years the water quality had improved so much that the lake was restocked with fish, and people could go swimming. It could even supply drinking water.

Today, the biggest stress to ecosystems is global warming. Our planet's atmospheric temperature is rising. If this continues, it may affect all Earth's ecosystems. By disrupting the whole world, global warming might cause a disaster that may take ecosystems hundreds of years to recover.

Ecosystem Recovers From a Volcano

Wind blows spiders into the area, and they die.

3

4

Decaying spiders release the nitrogen, oxygen, and carbon needed for living things. Their bodies start to create soil.

Everything in the ecosystem leaves or dies.

2

5

Wind and water erosion break down lava to form new soil.

The volcano erupts, burying everything under ashes, lava, and mud.

1

6

Wind blows seeds into the area. They take root and grow.

Geography

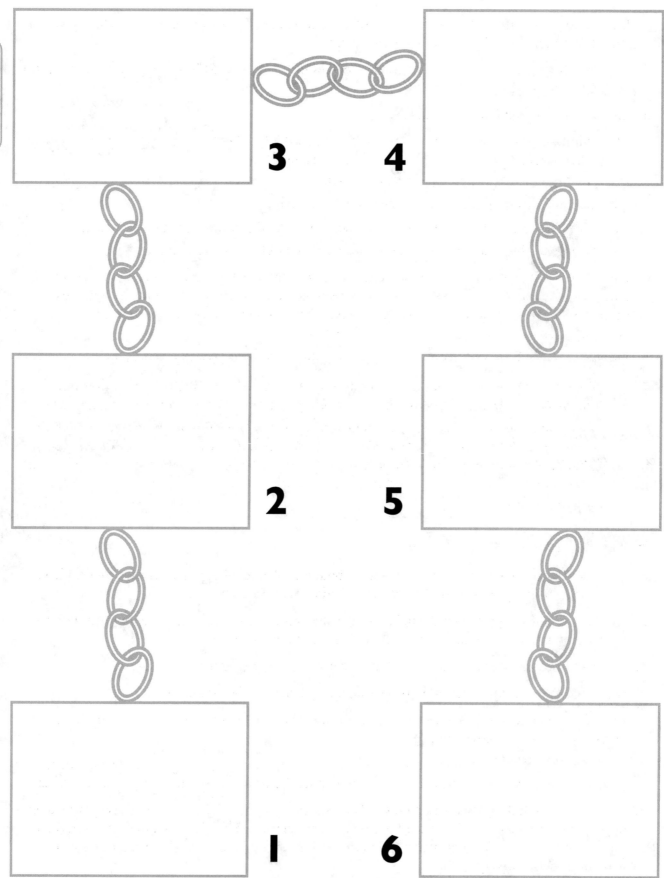

Day 1

1. Explain to your students that architecture often reflects the beliefs of its builders. Thus, you can learn things about a culture from its architecture.

2. Make an overhead transparency and student copies of "The Great Mosque at Samarra and the Taj Mahal" on page 62.

3. Introduce any unfamiliar vocabulary:

   ❖ **Islam**—a religion that started about 630 C.E. by the Prophet Muhammed; his followers are called Muslims and they believe in one god (named Allah)

   ❖ **Qur'an** (ku RAHN)— the holy book of Islam

   ❖ **mosque**—a place of prayer and worship for Muslims

   ❖ **minaret**—prayer tower; if standing alone, it must be the tallest structure in the area

   ❖ **geometric designs**—patterns based on shapes such as rectangles and triangles

4. Distribute the student copies. It is written at a 6.6 reading level, but the text is dense, so you may wish to read the article as a class. After reading, you may choose to show them photos of the Great Mosque and the Taj Mahal. Many pictures of these sites are available in books or encyclopedias and on the Web (do an image search).

5. Discuss the appearance of the Great Mosque and the Taj Mahal. Ask the following:

   • What conclusions can you draw about Islamic architecture? (*Muslims use minarets and onion-shaped domes. They use geometric designs in buildings and for decorations, etc.*)

   • Where are you most likely to see Islamic architecture? (*Muslims make up nearly ¹/₅ of the world's population, and over 50 nations have Muslim majority populations. The largest Muslim population resides in Indonesia. Millions of Muslims live in Middle Eastern nations, Bangladesh, Pakistan, India, Turkey, the Turkic Central Asian republics, China, and Sub-Saharan Africa.*)

Day 2

1. Explain to students that a lot of information about the Islamic religion that can be gleaned from this article. Their goal is to find eight major understandings about Muslims.

2. Display the transparency of the article. As the students suggest ideas, underscore them with an overhead pen while the students use highlighters on their copies.

3. Make an overhead transparency and student copies of the organizer on page 64.

4. Distribute the student copies and display the transparency of the organizer.

5. As a class, transfer the information from the article onto the lines of the web; the completed graphic organizer is shown on page 63.

6. At the bottom of the web, there is space to write some questions. Ask the students what questions they have about Muslims and Islam after completing the web. These questions go on the lines.

7. You can research the answers as a class. This is a great opportunity for you to show your students how to find answers quickly on the Internet or in an encyclopedia. It's important to discuss the search term (keyword) under which to look for information. If one search term doesn't work, what others can they try?

The Great Mosque at Samarra and the Taj Mahal

Architecture often reflects the beliefs of its builders. Muslim builders use minarets, domes, and geometric and floral designs. They use designs because their religion does not allow them to create images of human beings or their god, Allah. Two examples of Islamic architecture are the Great Mosque at Samarra in Iraq and Taj Mahal in India.

Most people living in Iraq are Muslims. A mosque is an Islamic place of worship. One of the most famous is the Great Mosque of Samarra. It is near the Tigris River north of Baghdad, Iraq. Construction on it started about 820 and ended in 851 C.E. Made of baked brick, at that time it was the largest mosque on Earth. It has an elegant spiral design unlike later mosques.

Another mosque is on the grounds of the Taj Mahal. It is the world's most famous tomb. The Indian ruler Shah Jahan had it built for his favorite wife, Mumtaz Mahal. The tomb stands on the River Yamuna in Agra, India. It took 20,000 workers to build it. They labored for two decades—from 1632 until 1653 C.E.

Large gardens laid out in geometric designs surround the Taj Mahal. They look like a beautiful Persian rug. Red sandstone walls enclose the gardens and other structures near the Taj Mahal. There are several watchtowers. The main gate has verses from the Qur'an, which is the holy book of Islam. It contains Allah's words and was written by the Prophet Muhammed about 630 C.E.

The Taj Mahal itself is made of white marble. It stands on a red sandstone base. At each corner of this base stands a tall, thin minaret. A minaret is a prayer tower that is built taller than nearby structures. Five times each day the call to prayer comes from atop minarets. Like most minarets, an onion-shaped dome tops each graceful spire. A similar dome rests over the center of the Taj Mahal. Four smaller domes surround it. Verses from the Qur'an decorate the outer walls. These walls have geometric and floral designs inlaid with semiprecious gems, too. The tomb's main room has two monuments. Beneath them lie the bodies of Shah Jahan and his wife. Each monument has elaborate carvings and inlaid gems.

When the Taj Mahal was built, many Muslims lived in India. In the 1940s most Indian Muslims moved to Pakistan, leaving Hindus in the majority in India. This division remains today.

Taj Mahal

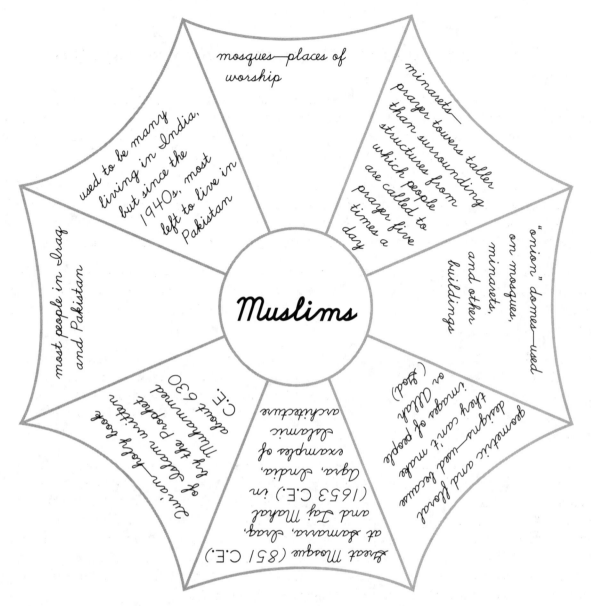

1. *How and why did the Prophet Muhammed start the religion of Islam?*

   About 610 C.E. Muhammed began receiving visitations from the angel Gabriel sent by Allah. He was told to write down Allah's words to share with others.

2. *Why did most of the Indian Muslims move to Pakistan in the 1940s?*

   The Indian Muslims felt that the Hindu government discriminated against them. It was agreed that they could form their own nation (Pakistan) if they moved north. So Hindus left the area that would become Pakistan and moved south, and Muslims left India and moved north.

3. *How many Muslims are there worldwide?*

   1.1 billion. It's the second most populous world religion (after Christianity).

Geography

1. _____

_____

_____

2. _____

_____

_____

3. _____

_____

_____

1. Discuss what a myth is (*a legend, usually concerning some hero or event, especially one that is concerned with gods and explains some practice, rite, or natural phenomenon*) and why ancient peoples created them (*to explain nature; to solidify collective beliefs; to justify social institutions*)

2. Make student copies of "Pandora's Box" on page 66.

3. Make an overhead transparency and student copies of the "Greek Temple" graphic organizer on page 68.

4. Introduce any unfamiliar vocabulary:

   ✧ **intrigued**—fascinated; aroused curiosity

   ✧ **humanity**—humankind; the human race

   ✧ **pitiful**—sad, pathetic

   ✧ **hideous**—ugly, repulsive, monstrous

   ✧ **misery**—suffering

   ✧ **despair**—without hope; hopelessness

5. Have the students independently read "Pandora's Box." Since it is written at a 4.2 reading level, it should be accessible to most class members.

6. Reconvene the class and discuss the myth. As this myth was told repeatedly, what values and beliefs were being reinforced in Greek citizens' minds?

   • Zeus was the chief god in charge of other gods.

   • Epimetheus created all living creatures except for humans.

   • Prometheus made the first human man; Zeus made the first human woman.

   • The world was originally a paradise where no one died.

   • Evil came into the world through the rash actions of Pandora, the first woman.

   • Hope also entered the world through Pandora's actions.

7. Display the overhead of the "Greek Temple." As a class, establish the main idea. You may need to build this idea on a blank transparency before you come up with the final statements: *When Pandora opened her box, she released all the world's evils. Then she released hope to keep people from total despair.* Write the main idea across the top of the temple.

8. Ask individual students to provide details from the story to fill in the columns of the organizer.

9. See if your class can draw comparisons between the Greek myth and the Judeo-Christian story of Adam and Eve in the Garden of Eden (*all creatures were created before man; woman was created immediately after man; no one had to die in the beginning of the world; evil entered the world through the rash actions of a woman; etc.*)

Extension: Put students into groups of three and ask them to develop and then write a new myth explaining a different theory about how the negative things mentioned in Pandora's box (disease, war, death) came to be. They can take turns writing paragraphs or even sentences. You may want to let them decide which way they want to do it.

Reading

Pandora's Box

Zeus was king, the chief god on Mount Olympus. All other gods and goddesses followed his commands. Soon after the beginning of the world, Zeus told Epimetheus to make living creatures. Epimetheus was delighted. He made turtles and horses, lions and fish. He fashioned snails and sheep and snakes and bees. Then Epimetheus's brother, Prometheus, used mud and water to make a man. He gave him arms and legs and hair. Prometheus had made a human that looked like a god. This made Zeus furious. He sent Prometheus away.

But Zeus was intrigued as well as angered by Prometheus's creation. So he created another mud creature. This one was a woman. He made her beautiful, clever, and talented. Zeus named her Pandora and gave her to Epimetheus as his bride. He also gave the happy couple an odd wedding gift. It was a locked wooden chest. Zeus warned them never to open the box or humanity would be forever sorry.

Epimetheus was glad to follow Zeus's order, but Pandora longed to know what was in the box. After all, it was her wedding gift. So one day while Epimetheus was out, she felt curious. She went over to the box. To her shock, she heard pitiful voices coming from within it. They pleaded with her to set them free.

She covered her ears, but they cried all the louder: "Please let us out, Pandora! We are trapped in here—you must set us free . . . Oh, please, Pandora!" Pandora cried, "But I can't! I have no way to open the box!"

Then one of the voices whispered, "The key is in the lock." And sure enough, it had magically appeared. Pandora turned the key and heard the latch click. WHAM! The lid flew open with a fierce blast that knocked Pandora backwards. Shrieking, snarling, hideous spirits flew from the box. Each wicked spirit shouted its name.

"I am Disease," said one.

"I'm Cruelty," said the next.

"I'm Pain, and she's Sorrow," said another.

"I'm Hatred, and he's War."

"I'm Jealousy, Envy, and Greed."

And the final, most terrifying one of all cried, "I am Death!"

The terrible spirits flew out Pandora's window and infected the world. Never again would the Earth be the wonderful, happy, deathless place it had been at the start of creation. Pandora, horrified by what she had done, slammed the lid shut. Then she heard another tiny voice from within. "No, don't leave me in here, Pandora! That would be an even worse mistake than opening the box in the first place. I am Hope. Without me, no one can bear the misery you have released."

So Pandora opened the lid and set free the tiny white butterfly named Hope. It flapped its tiny wings and followed the horrors out her window. As it fluttered around the world, it kept people from utter despair.

When Pandora opened her wedding box, she released all the evils of the world. Then she released hope to keep people from total despair.

Zeus, the head god, created Pandora and gave her to Epimetheus as his bride.

Zeus gave the couple a locked box and told them never to open it.

Epimetheus was content to ignore the box, but Pandora's curiosity got the better of her.

After Pandora opened the box and saw that she'd released the world's evils, she regretted what she'd done.

Reading

Day 1

1. Prior to this lesson your students should be familiar with these figurative language devices: metaphor, simile, allusion, and onomatopoeia. Have the definition of these terms posted or recorded in the students' journals.

   ✧ **allusion**—someone or something mentioned through hints; usually about people, places, and things well known to the general public

   ✧ **metaphor**—a comparison of two things to show their similarity

   ✧ **simile**—a comparison of two things to show their similarity that uses the words *like* or *as*

   ✧ **onomatopoeia**—a word formed to sound like the noise it describes (*sizzle, rumble,* etc.)

2. Explain to the class that you are going to analyze a passage filled with figurative language. Introduce any unfamiliar vocabulary:

   ✧ **dilemma**—a difficult situation requiring a choice between equally undesirable options

   ✧ **bearings**—relative position

   ✧ **concussion**—injury to the brain due to jarring from a blow or fall, often resulting in a brief loss of consciousness

3. Make student copies of "Kevin's Dilemma" on page 70. Explain that the famous sculpture shown at the bottom is Auguste Rodin's *The Thinker*, which is referred to in the passage.

4. Make an overhead transparency and student copies of the "Classification Chart" graphic organizer on page 72.

5. Have the students silently read "Kevin's Dilemma." Since it is written at a 4.3 reading level, it should be accessible to most class members.

6. As a class, discuss the phrases in boldface. Ask your students which of the four types of figurative language each one demonstrates.

7. Display the transparency and distribute the student copies of the graphic organizer. Fill in the words *allusion, metaphor, onomatopoeia*, and *simile*. Ask students to provide one of each different type of figurative language. They fill in their charts while you do so on the overhead.

8. Have your students complete the graphic organizer independently for homework.

Day 2

1. Have students exchange their completed graphic organizers. Display the completed classification chart on the overhead and have the students mark each other's papers. Collect the homework.

2. Prior to this lesson, identify examples of figurative language from a novel that the class is currently reading. Mark them with sticky notes. Have the students turn to the designated pages and scan for the example of a figurative language device you name.

Extension: Pair the students and ask them to create a five-paragraph passage that includes one example each of metaphor, simile, allusion, and onomatopoeia.

Note: The "Classification Chart" graphic organizer can be adapted to other content area topics.

Reading

Kevin's Dilemma

Kevin kept **his eyes glued to the trail** his dad had taken up the mountain, wishing he would appear. His father had promised not to go to the summit without Kevin. He said that he was just going to scout ahead and get their bearings. But he had been gone far too long. Scouting around should have taken him no more than half an hour. Kevin wished he had a watch. **Time dragged so slowly that he felt he'd waited for days.**

Now the sun was sinking lower in the sky. Kevin licked his lips nervously and paced **as if he were a tiger in a cage.** He had promised his father that he'd stay put, but should he keep that promise? What if his dad was in trouble? Had he gotten hurt? Was he lying somewhere in agony, hoping that Kevin would find him? Or was this just another one of his father's empty promises—**another link in his long chain of broken vows?**

Perhaps he didn't believe that Kevin could climb the ropes at the end of the trail to reach the summit. After several of the steepest inclines, he'd asked Kevin if he felt up to continuing. Maybe he thought **Kevin was such a mouse** that he'd gone to the summit alone and when he returned he'd tell his son that the trail looked too dangerous for them to continue. Kevin didn't know what to think.

Kevin flung himself down on a large stone near the edge of the path and, resting his chin on his fist, gave a big sigh. A smile briefly lit his face as he realized that **he must look like Rodin's famous statue,** *The Thinker*. Then he frowned and shook his head. This was no time to be thinking about sculpture! He had better figure out what to do, and fast. **The sun wouldn't slow its pace for him.** He had to be a thinker rather than look like one.

He stamped his right foot impatiently, **crunching** small sticks beneath his heel. His stomach **grumbled** with hunger, reminding him that he hadn't eaten for hours. How much time had actually passed? How much longer should he keep waiting? Should he go up the trail or go back? **He felt as befuddled as when he'd gotten a concussion** after falling off his skateboard. How could he possibly make the right decision without all the facts? If his dad were injured, it would be best to go for help. He knew that he was too slight and his father too stocky for Kevin to rescue him. **Jack might as well have tried to carry the giant down the beanstalk.**

Sample Graphic Organizer

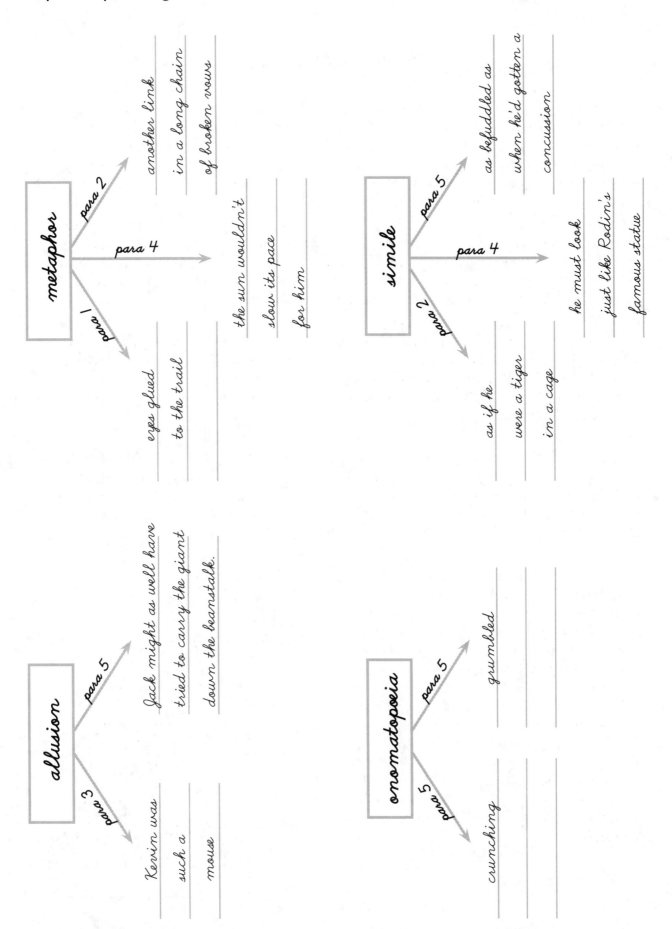

©Teacher Created Resources, Inc.

71   #8096 Content Area Lessons Using Graphic Organizers

Reading

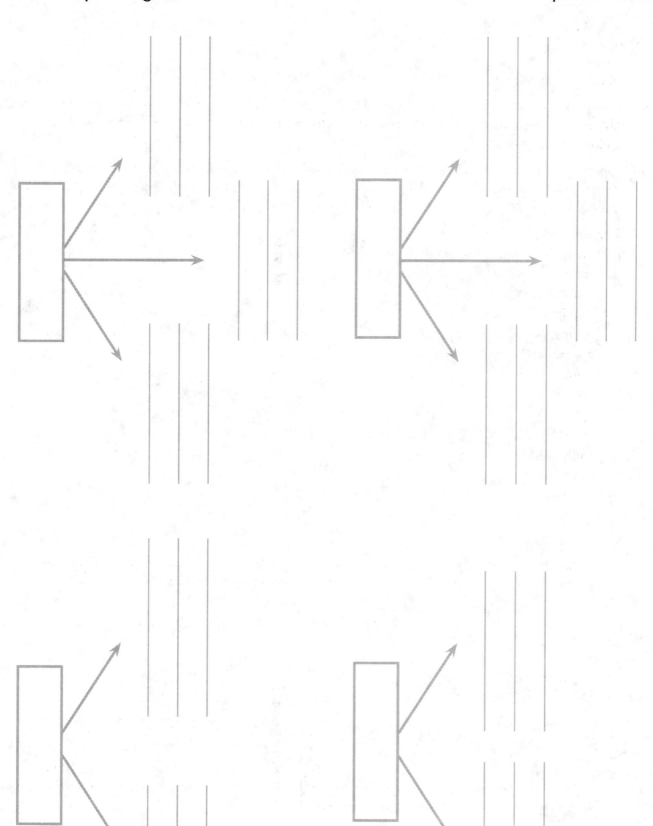

Day 1

1. Make student copies of "Famous Poems About Nature" on page 74.

2. Introduce couplet poetry by reading the poem "Trees." Ask your students to use context to figure out the meaning of the words *bosom* (referring to the breast as the center of feelings or emotions) and *intimately* (having a close relationship).

3. Explain that poetry often has meter (*a rhythm made by a specific number of syllables*) and rhyme. "Trees" is a couplet. Reread the poem chorally. Then ask your students if they can figure out the definition of a couplet (*every pair of lines rhyme and have eight syllables*).

4. Introduce any unfamiliar vocabulary:
   - **yonder**—distant but within sight
   - **medley**—a mixture or combination
   - **rubbish bag**—trash bag
   - **rovings**—travels
   - **worsted**—wool cloth that is woven from yarn and has a hard, smooth surface and no nap
   - **compacted**—pressed tightly
   - **cunningly**—cleverly
   - **renowned**—famous
   - **pray**—the archaic meaning of this word is "please"
   - **contrive**—to plan with ingenuity to bring to fruition a plan or scheme
   - **aghast** (uh-GAST)—shocked
   - **vowed**—sworn
   - **ne'er**—abbreviation of "never" to make it one syllable

5. Read the second poem on page 74, "A Sparrow's Nest." Have students take turns reading each pair of rhyming lines.

6. Ask your class if the poem is in couplets. (*Yes, it is.*) Ask how it differs from the definition of couplet we surmised from "Trees." (*Not all of the lines have identical syllables—for example, the first two lines are six and eight syllables respectively*). Revise the class definition of *couplet* (see the definition on page 75). Post it in a prominent spot.

Day 2

1. Make an overhead transparency and student copies of the organizer on page 76.

2. Have your students get out the "Famous Poems About Nature" page. Display the transparency and distribute the student copies.

3. As a class, fill in the "Poetry Analysis" graphic organizer (a completed one is on page 75) for "Trees." Ask them what kind of tree they should draw in the illustration section. (The tree should be deciduous, because that's indicated in the poem.)

4. Pass out new student copies of the graphic organizer. They are to independently fill it out for "A Sparrow's Nest." There aren't enough example spaces, so they can pick the six pairs of rhyming lines they like most. Their illustration must include details (such as the colors of the fabrics) from the poem. If necessary, they can complete this assignment for homework.

5. Collect the completed graphic organizers to check for understanding.

Famous Poems About Nature

Trees
by Joyce Kilmer

I think that I shall never see
A poem as lovely as a tree.
A tree whose hungry mouth is pressed
Against the sweet earth's flowing breast;
A tree that looks at God all day,
And lifts her leafy arms to pray;
A tree that may in summer wear
A nest of robins in her hair;
Upon whose bosom snow has lain;
Who intimately lives with rain.
Poems are made by fools like me,
But only God can make a tree.

The Sparrow's Nest
by Mary Howitt

Just look what I have found!
A Sparrow's nest upon the ground.
A Sparrow's nest as you may see,
blown out of yonder old elm tree.
And what a medley thing it is!
I never saw a nest like this.
Not neatly wove with decent care
of silvery moss and shining hair.
But put together, odds and ends,
picked up from enemies and friends.
See, bits of thread, and bits of rag,
just like a little rubbish bag!
Here is a scrap of red and brown
like the old washer-woman's gown.
And here is muslin, pink and green
and bits of calico between.
See, hair of dog and fur of cat
and rovings of a worsted mat;
And threads of silks, and many a feather,
compacted cunningly together.
Had these odds and ends been brought
to some wise man renowned for thought,
Some man—of men a very gem—
pray, what could he have done with them?
If we had said, "Here, sir, we bring
you many a worthless little thing.
Just bits and scraps, so very small
that they have scarcely size at all.
And out of these, you must contrive
a dwelling large enough for five;
Neat, warm, and snug with comfort stored
for five small things to lodge and board."
How would the man of learning vast,
have been astonished and aghast!
And vowed that such a thing had been
ne'er heard of, thought of, much less seen!

Title: Trees

By: Joyce Kilmer

Type: couplet

Examples

Examples

I think that I
shall never see

A poem as lovely
as a tree.

A tree that may in
summer wear

A nest of robins in
her hair . . .

A tree whose hungry
mouth is pressed

Against the sweet
earth's flowing
breast . . .

Definition: A couplet
is two lines of verse
that rhyme and
have a similar meter
(number of syllables).

Upon whose bosom
snow has lain;

Who intimately
lives with rain.

A tree that looks at
God all day,

And lifts her leafy
arms to pray . . .

Poems are made by
fools like me,

But only God can
make a tree.

Illustration

Reading

Title:

By:

Type:

Examples   **Examples**

Definition:

Illustration

Reading

Day 1

1. See if your students can define a fact (*something that can be proven*) and an opinion (*what someone thinks or believes; a judgment*).

2. Write this story on the board or overhead without the letters in parentheses:

   Wendy looked out the window and said, "Look! It's snowing." (**F**) Katie rushed over to the window and said, "That's terrific!" (**O**) "No, it's not," said Ken. (**O**) Mr. Carter told them to take their seats. (**F**) Then he said, "They're forecasting six inches by tomorrow morning." (**F & O**—*It's a fact that that's the forecast, but the actual amount of snow accumulation is the educated opinion of the forecasters.*)

3. Have your students read the story, and then ask them to identify facts and opinions sentence by sentence. Discuss why each is a fact or opinion. Make sure you stress that statements are not facts just because you agree with them—a common error with this age group.

4. As a class, brainstorm words that indicate that something is an opinion (*believes, thinks, best, worst, should, ought to, better, more, terrific, awful,* etc.). Leave this list posted.

5. Make student copies of "Distinguishing Between Facts and Opinions" on page 78.

6. Have the students read the passage and complete the questions at the bottom of the page independently. As soon as your students finish working, go over the answers:
   1. O (*the words "should have" indicate that the writer believes this is true; not everyone believes in vaccinations for children*)
   2. F (*something stated in a law can be verified*)
   3. F (*this can be verified in many ways*)
   4. O (*"must" indicates an opinion that many—but not all—share*)
   5. F (*this can be verified*)
   6. O (*"is better than" indicates that this is an opinion*)

Day 2

1. Write these statements on the board. Do not include the letters in parentheses:
   1. America declared its independence from Britain on July 4, 1776. (F)
   2. The trucks Ford makes are better than the ones Toyota makes. (O)
   3. Rhode Island is the smallest state. (F)
   4. People will never live on Mars. (O)

2. Make an overhead transparency and two copies for each student of the organizer on page 81.

3. Distribute one copy of the graphic organizer to each student. Have them write the numbers for the factual statements on the board on the "Facts" side of the scale and the numbers for the opinion statements on the "Opinions" side of the scale. Do the first two together to be sure they understand.

4. Allow two minutes for this task. Display the transparency and fill it in with the answers the students provide. Be sure they can explain their answers.

5. Make student copies of the editorial on page 79. Distribute the second copy of the graphic organizer. Pair the students. Have them read and discuss the editorial, then write the number of each statement on the appropriate side of the scale.

6. Wipe the transparency clean and display it. As a class, go over the editorial and weighing which statements are facts and which are opinions.

Reading

Distinguishing Between Facts and Opinions

When you read nonfiction, you need to be able to distinguish between facts and opinions. A fact is something that is true and can be proven. You could check a source (such an encyclopedia, an almanac or other reference book, the Internet, etc.) and find the same information. Examples of facts may be dates, numbers, and names.

- The American Civil War lasted four years.

- On December 7, 1941, the Japanese bombed Pearl Harbor.

No one should disagree with a fact because it can be proven to be true. But an opinion is what the writer believes to be true. An opinion cannot be proven, so a person can disagree with it. Often a science theory—such as the universe began as the result of a big bang—is just an educated opinion. When you read an ad, you often read opinions such as "We have the best prices in town" and "Hurry in for a great deal."

- You'll be disappointed if you miss seeing the Northern Lights.

- Everyone likes visiting New York City.

Unfortunately it's not always easy to determine which statements are facts and which are opinions. Here are some opinions that could be mistaken for facts:

- There is no Loch Ness Monster. (*No one knows if there is one or not. There is no absolute proof one way or the other.*)

- Dinosaurs died when a meteor hit the Earth. (*No one knows for sure why they died.*)

- Global warming will end life on our planet. (*No one knows for certain what the long-term results of global warming will be.*)

Especially in science and politics, opinions can be hard to detect! Even editorials may have more facts than opinions. So when you read nonfiction, think about the whole article. Is the writer saying that he or she is sure about something? Or is the writer stating a theory?

Try this: If the statement is a fact, circle "F." If the statement is an opinion, circle "O."

For opinions, underline the word(s) that let you know they are opinions.

F O 1. Children should have the full series of shots before going to school.

F O 2. The law states your child must have the full series of shots to go to school.

F O 3. Mammals are warm-blooded animals.

F O 4. We must pass laws to protect endangered mammals.

F O 5. Nuclear fission can make electrical power.

F O 6. Nuclear power is better than coal-generated electric power.

Editorial

The author of this editorial supported it with facts he found through research. For this assignment, you can assume that the facts he has included are definitely facts. Therefore, read closely to determine which statements are his opinions.

Dear Editor:

Almost no one realizes that food corporations have changed our crops.[1] Genes from bacteria, viruses, and foreign plants have been added to corn, soybeans, squash, tomatoes, and potatoes.[2] More than 60 percent of the packaged foods in U.S. stores has at least one gene-altered ingredient.[3] They're hard to avoid.[4] About 50 percent of all canola plants, 40 percent of all soybeans, and 20 percent of all corn grown in the U.S. and Canada have had their genes altered.[5] Both nations' governments let these grains be mixed with normal grains and sold without labeling.[6] Yet there has not been even one health safety test.[7]

To make insect-resistant corn, the companies added a gene from BT, an insect-killing bacteria.[8] Now every cell of the plant has BT toxin in it.[9] And BT kills good insects like Monarch butterflies and ladybugs.[10]

If that doesn't shock you, think about this: genes put into a plant can cause it to form new proteins.[11] No studies have been done to see whether these new proteins cause problems in humans. [12] There has been a big rise in soybean allergies in the past few years.[13] I believe this is due to a new protein.[14]

You should help us to stop the spread of gene-altered foods.[15] Everyone should tell the supermarkets to ban products that have gene-altered ingredients.[16] They should buy only products with certified organic ingredients.[17] If we won't buy gene-altered produce, the food corporations will pay attention.[18] They must stop the gene-altering, at least until safety tests have been done.[19]

Noah Grinderson, Ph.D.

Noah Grinderson, Ph.D.

Association for Natural Produce

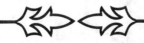

Reading

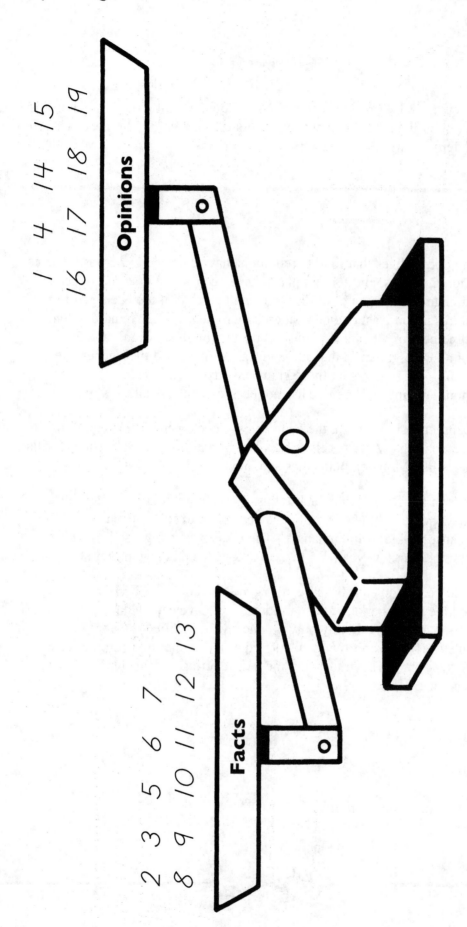

Opinions

1 4 14 15
16 17 18 19

Facts

2 3 5 6 7
8 9 10 11 12 13

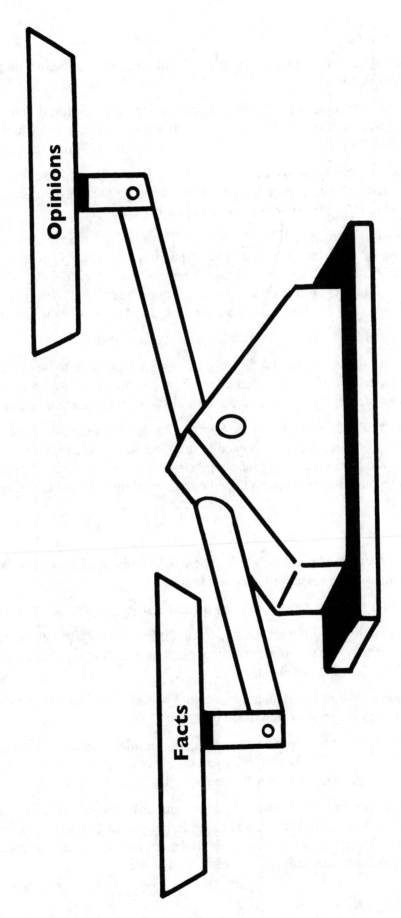

Day 1

1. This lesson is meant to follow the lesson on facts and opinions that begins on page 77. However, it can be done independently.

2. If you have not already done so, distribute student copies of the editorial on page 79. Have your students read it and help them to identify which statements are facts and which are opinions. The answer key is shown on the completed "Weighing the Facts" graphic organizer on page 80.

3. Note that the majority of the editorial's statements are facts. Therefore, even when writing something persuasive like an editorial, it should be based on facts. Noah Grinderson used facts to help persuade his readers to agree with and act upon his opinion.

4. Make an overhead transparency of the completed "Pen Plan" graphic organizer on page 83. Before displaying it, cover the "My goal" line. Then have the students read the statements on the transparency. After reading the entire graphic organizer, ask your students: "What does it appear that this author will be trying to persuade his or her audience to do?" (*to recycle every possible thing*) How do you know? (*That's the common thread in the facts the writer gathered.*)

5. Reveal the "My goal" line. Ask, "How closely did the author stick to his or her goal?"

6. Be sure to point out to your class that the very first fact would have to be modified after the author investigated to find out which agency in his or her own area should be contacted. Then the author might even include the phone number or website of the agency in the editorial.

7. As a whole class, create an editorial on the board using the facts that the writer included on the "Pen Plan." Check off each fact as it is used in the "Included" column. Your class may choose not to include all the facts on the graphic organizer. If so, that's a perfect opportunity to discuss how writers sift through information and decide to leave things out as they compose and revise.

Days 2–5

1. Each student picks a topic about which he or she would like to write an editorial. You may want to do a class brainstorming session to generate topics.

2. Make student copies of the organizer on page 84 and distribute them to the students.

3. Have students research four different sources to find information they can use to persuade others in their editorial. If they use websites, briefly explain how to find reputable sites. Students then fill in the "Pen Plan" graphic organizer.

4. Be sure your students follow the steps in the writing process; you may want to check their graphic organizers before they begin their first draft.

5. Use the students' editorials to create a class newsletter entitled "Since You Want My Opinion" and make copies for the entire class. Have them take the newsletters home to be signed by their parents. This encourages them to share the project with their families.

Note: The "Pen Plan" graphic organizer can be used with any kind of writing (to inform, to entertain, to persuade). Even a lot of fiction is based largely on facts (unless it's fantasy). Using this with other writing assignments will help your students to see how real writers work by doing research on which they base their articles, editorials, and stories.

My goal: *to persuade the readers to recycle everything that they can*

Included	Facts	Source
	Some things you can recycle require special handling procedures and special recycling places or events. Just ask your local recycling office (city, county, or state) for information. Don't throw away anything that can be recycled! Recycled soda bottles can be made into T-shirts, combs, fleece blankets, and computer keyboards.	National Institute of Environmental Health Sciences Kid's Page website
	Once glass, metal, and plastic enter a landfill, the resources are stuck there. Things rot slowly in landfills and landfills are sealed, so nutrients don't return to the soil like they should. We are running out of landfill space. Paper takes up the most landfill space. The amount of solid waste produced in the U.S.A. increases each year.	World Book Encyclopedia on CD-ROM, 2007.
	Even shiny wrapping paper, gable-top cartons, old cell phones, empty printer ink cartridges, waste oil, and automotive batteries can be recycled. Most of these items must be dropped off at a recycling location instead of going into a recycle bin.	Pennsylvania Department of Environmental Protection website
	Right now, just 32 percent of all solid waste is recycled, 14 percent is burned, and 54 percent goes into landfills. In 1996, recycling of solid waste in the United States prevented the release of 33 million tons of carbon into the air—about the amount emitted annually by 25 million cars!	U.S. Environmental Protection Agency website

Writing

My goal: _____

Included	Facts	Source

Writing

Day 1

1. Make student copies of "Transitional Devices: The Glue That Puts Thoughts Together" on page 86. Read the page together and discuss the examples given. Point out that sometimes the transitional device is at the start, the middle, and the end. It all depends upon where it works best.

2. Draw the analogy that building a sentence is like an equation: you add up the parts to create a whole.

3. Write these sentences on the board, but do not include the transitional devices shown in parentheses:

   - The mother crocodile stays close. She hears her babies' cries. She digs up the eggs. (*nearby/when*)

   - Most of Holland's land lies below sea level. Water seeps back in. Pumping is done each day. (*thus/so/therefore/as a result*)

   - The dik-dik is the smallest antelope. An adult weighs just 6 to 8 pounds. (*since/because*)

4. Make an overhead transparency and student copies of the "It All Adds Up" graphic organizer on page 88.

5. As a class, have your students select a word or phrase from the "Transitional Devices" paper that will link the thoughts together. Write the sentence components, including the transitional device in the boxes of the equation. Put a star in the boxes containing the transitional devices. When possible, discuss different configurations to see which one sounds the best. Go with what the students choose, unless it's clearly wrong.

6. Be sure to discuss appropriate internal and terminal punctuation. Sample answers appear on the completed graphic organizer on page 87.

Day 2

1. Write these sentences on the board, but do not include the transitional devices shown in parentheses—they're for your information:

   - The men within the fort held fast. It was an awful ordeal. They were cold, hungry, sick, and lacked supplies. (*but/however/yet/because/since*)

   - A female cheetah gives birth to two to eight cubs. Nine out of every 10 die within the first three months. (*although/but/yet/however*)

   - He searched along the roadside until he found a stout pole. He tied the horse's front and back legs together. He tied the horse upside down to the pole. (*next/then/finally*)

2. Make and distribute new student copies of the graphic organizer.

3. Pair the students and have them use the page about transitional devices and the sentences from the board to fill in the graphic organizer. They should discuss the transitional device and where it would best go to join the information. Have each pair complete individual graphic organizers and submit them to you.

Writing

Transitional Devices:
The Glue That Puts Thoughts Together

Transitional devices are words and phrases that "glue" thoughts together. Without the use of transitional devices, your writing will be choppy. Use them to combine thoughts to build interesting compound and complex sentences.

To signal cause and effect

Words: *consequently; therefore; as a result; because; thus; if . . . then*

Example: There are too few schools and teachers, and many parents educate their sons but not their daughters. As a result, just a little over half of all Liberian adults can read and write.

To indicate sequence

Words: *furthermore; in addition; first, second, third; finally; again; also; too; besides; last; next; then; eventually*

Example: Around 1000 AD, Leif Ericsson landed in Canada and named it Vinland. Then he returned to Norway and told others about the place. The next year, Norse men and women set off to start a settlement in the new land.

To signal comparison

Words: *similarly; also; in the same way; although; even though; at the same time; but; even so; however; nevertheless; still; yet; on the other hand*

Example: Americans have freedom of choice, even though that means that they may sometimes make bad decisions.

To give an example

Words: *for example; for instance; in fact; indeed; of course; specifically; which means; to illustrate; as a matter of fact*

Example: Based on its content, a nonfiction book gets assigned a Dewey Decimal number. For example, books about pets have the Dewey Decimal number 636.

To explain a reason

Words: *for this reason; to this end; with this in mind; for this purpose; consequently; therefore; thus*

Example: Our ship is believed to be in European waters; consequently, we can approach an enemy vessel without causing suspicion.

To show time

Words: *before; after; later; afterward; immediately; in the meantime; meanwhile; now; since; soon; then; ever since then; while; when; during that time*

Example: The near-drowning experience had terrified her. Ever since then, she had been afraid to go in the water.

To give location

Words: *nearby; above; below; beyond; farther; here; opposite to; over there*

Example: I pointed and said, "I swear that just minutes ago I saw the old wagon over there."

The mother crocodile stays nearby + and when she hears her babies' cries + she digs up the eggs =

The mother crocodile stays nearby, and when she hears her babies' cries, she digs up the eggs.

Most of Holland's land lies below sea level + therefore, water seeps backs in, and + as a result, pumping is done each day =

Most of Holland's land lies below sea level; therefore, water seeps back in, and as a result, pumping is done each day.

Since + an adult weighs just 6 to 8 pounds + the dik-dik is the smallest antelope =

Since an adult weighs just 6 to 8 pounds, the dik-dik is the smallest antelope.

Writing

||　　　　　　　||　　　　　　　||

+　　　　　　　+　　　　　　　+

+　　　　　　　+　　　　　　　+

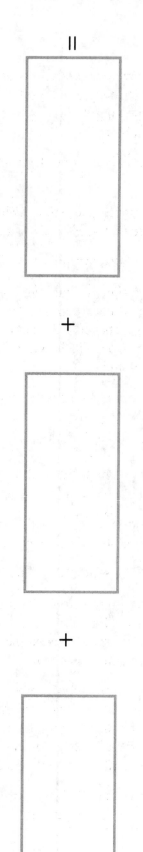

Days 1–2

1. Decide how you want your students to cite information sources. Your district may have an established style or a preference for APA or MLA style. Prepare, display, and distribute a guide showing them how to cite information found in an encyclopedia, a website, and a nonfiction book.

2. Have available in your classroom or library a set of encyclopedias, biographies, and Internet access.

3. Demonstrate to your students how to look up information in an encyclopedia (using guide words) and online (using a search engine and keywords).

4. Show your students how to write a citation for the information you found.

5. You can assign or allow your students to choose a person about whom they would like to write a short composition. The end product will be four to five paragraphs and will cover important facts about the person's life and actions. They should make a two-column chart on a piece of paper. They write the facts in the first column and the citation for the source in the second column.

6. Provide your students with time and opportunity to access resource materials.

Day 3

1. Make an overhead transparency of the completed graphic organizer on page 91. Display it for the class. Discuss the sentences and how each one starts with a different letter of the alphabet. This adds variety to the sentences and makes for a more interesting composition.

2. Make and distribute student copies of the completed "Key Sentences" organizer on page 91.

3. Cut apart the sentences of the transparency. Have your class do the same at their desks.

4. As a class, go through and move the sentences around to find a logical sequence for the information. First, have students suggest which sentences go together. Group them together on the overhead screen. Next, have the students determine the order of the paragraphs. Last, have the students decide the order of the sentences within each paragraph.

5. Emphasize throughout the process the importance of flexibility. Real authors edit and revise constantly. They move paragraphs around, and they move sentences from one paragraph to another. Encourage your students to do the same. Although they assigned a sentence to one paragraph, that does not mean it has to go there. Too often students are rigid in their writing, and their creativity and the quality of their final work reflects this.

6. Last of all, number the sentences in an appropriate order. After determining the correct order, discuss again if the paragraphs are in logical order.

Writing

7. The composition should read like this:

> Crescent Beach, Florida, is the birthplace of one of the most influential people in the American labor movement. Born in 1889, Asa Philip Randolph became a leader in the struggle for laborers' rights during the first half of the 20th century.
>
> During World War II, African-American workers were mistreated by the defense industry. They could not get jobs; or if they did have a job, they could not earn raises or promotions. Randolph asked President Franklin D. Roosevelt to put a stop to the discrimination against black workers. Yet President Roosevelt did nothing. Outraged, Randolph threatened to fill the capital with 100,000 African Americans in a mass protest.
>
> So President Roosevelt established the Fair Employment Practices Committee. Employment discrimination was banned in the defense industry and government in June 1941 as a result of Randolph's efforts. No longer could jobs or promotions be withheld based on a person's race, creed, color, or national origin.
>
> Asa Philip Randolph was given the NAACP's highest award, the Spingarn Medal, in 1942. In 1957 the AFL-CIO, the largest American labor union, named Randolph its vice president. He died in 1979.

Days 4–5

1. Make student copies of the blank "Key Sentences" graphic organizer on page 92. Your students will put the information that they found for their person on this graphic organizer. The challenge is that each sentence must start with a different letter. Based on the needs of your class, set a minimum and maximum number of sentences (such as 9 to 15). There are 13 sentences in the example composition on Asa Philip Randolph.

2. Be sure to have the students show you their completed graphic organizer before they begin writing their compositions.

3. Have the students number their sentences (in pencil) in the order in which they think they will write them in the composition. Then pair the students and have them evaluate and discuss each other's sequence. Since it's in pencil, they can move things around.

4. Next, the students should independently make paragraphing decisions. Then each student should write or word-process a short report about his or her person. If handwritten, the citations for the information should go on the back of the same sheet. If the report is word-processed, the citations should go on a separate sheet entitled "Sources" or "References."

5. Collect and inspect both the reports and the graphic organizers.

Write sentences about your topic. Start each sentence with a different letter. Use words that start with "Ex" for the "X" sentence.

A	Asa Philip Randolph was given the NAACP's highest award, the Spingarn Medal, in 1942.
B	Born in 1889, Asa Philip Randolph became a leader in the struggle for laborers' rights during the first half of the 20th century.
C	Crescent Beach, Florida, is the birthplace of one of the most influential people in the American labor movement.
D	During World War II, African-American workers were mistreated by the defense industry.
E	Employment discrimination was banned in the defense industry and government in June 1941 as a result of Randolph's efforts.
F	
G	
H	He died in 1979.
I	In 1957 the AFL-CIO, the largest American labor union, named Randolph its vice president.
J	
K	
L	
M	
N	No longer could jobs, or promotions be withheld based on a person's race, creed, color, or national origin.
O	Outraged, Randolph threatened to fill the capital with 100,000 African Americans in a mass protest.
P	
Q	
R	Randolph asked President Franklin D. Roosevelt to put a stop to the discrimination against black workers.
S	So President Roosevelt established the Fair Employment Practices Committee.
T	They could not get jobs; or if they did have a job, they could not earn raises or promotions.
U	
V	
W	
EX	
Y	Yet President Roosevelt did nothing.
Z	

Writing

Write sentences about your topic. Start each sentence with a different letter. Use words that start with "Ex" for the "X" sentence.

A	
B	
C	
D	
E	
F	
G	
H	
I	
J	
K	
L	
M	
N	
O	
P	
Q	
R	
S	
T	
U	
V	
W	
EX	
Y	
Z	

Day 1

1. Ask your students to define *prefix* and offer words with prefixes. (*A prefix is a syllable added to the beginning of a word that changes its meaning or part of speech.*) List the words they suggest on the board. Draw conclusions about the meaning of a few common ones (such as *un-* and *re-*).

2. Ask your students to define *suffix* and offer words with suffixes. (*A suffix is a syllable added to the end of a word that changes its meaning or part of speech.*) List the words they suggest on the board. Draw conclusions about the meaning of a few common ones (such as *-less* and *-ful*).

3. Introduce the prefixes *in-* and *ir-*. Both mean "not." Introduce the suffixes *-ible* and *-able*. Both mean "capable of being."

4. Make and display an overhead transparency of the "Building Blocks" graphic organizer on page 96.

5. One at a time, write the given words on the completed graphic organizer on page 95, part by part. (in-divis-ible; ir-reverse-ible (drop the *e*); ir-repair-able (drop the *i*); in-ex-cuse-able (drop the *e*)) Show the students how to put the word parts together to form a word and write it on the line. Note when *e* is dropped from the base word. Discuss the meaning of each word and how you derived the meaning from its parts.

6. Ask for student volunteers to generate sentences for each of the words. Write them on a blank transparency.

7. Have the students choose two of the words just learned and write a sentence for each. Collect these papers to check for understanding.

Day 2

1. Write these words in parts on the organizer on page 96: *in-flex-ible; ir-retrieve-able; in-separable; ir-resist-ible.* You may want to put a star next to the blocks for *irretrievable* to indicate that they should drop the *e*. Then make copies and distribute them to the students.

2. Have the students join the word parts on the building blocks to form the complete words and write them in the place provided. The students then write the meaning of each based on the word parts (no dictionary use).

3. Have the students write a sentence for each of the words on the back of the paper. Collect and check for understanding.

4. Make student copies of "Working with Words" on page 94. Do the first two with the class. (*1. indigestible; 2. indescribable*) Have the students complete the page for homework.

Day 3

1. Have students exchange papers and correct the homework. (*3. invisible; 4. irresponsible; 5. irreplaceable; 6. inescapable*)

2. Discuss the meaning of each of the words on the "Building Blocks" graphic organizer the students completed. Read aloud a few of the best sentences generated by the students.

Note: What they've learned about the prefix *in-* holds true most of the time, but there are exceptions to the rule. Two are *invaluable* and *inflammable*. *Invaluable* means of great value, and *inflammable* means likely to catch on fire! (*Nonflammable* means "not apt to catch on fire.") Tell them to confidently use what they've learned but to double-check when they are unsure.

The prefixes *ir-* and *in-* mean "not."

The suffixes *-able* and *-ible* mean "capable of being."

irresponsible	**indescribable**	**irreplaceable**
inescapable	**invisible**	**indigestible**

Directions: Choose a word from the box to complete the sentence. Each word is used once.

1. Fiber is _____ ; it moves through the intestines without being broken down.

   _____ means _____

2. The girl's joy was _____ as she was reunited with her long-lost dog.

   _____ means _____

3. If that trophy was on the shelf, it must have been _____ , because I couldn't find it.

   _____ means _____

4. The _____ driver veered in and out of traffic lanes without signaling.

   _____ means _____

5. Since the rare doll was _____ , Sophia cried when she broke it.

   _____ means _____

6. Phil came to an _____ conclusion: he had to take the physics course in order to graduate.

   _____ means _____

prefix

base

suffix

indivisible

means

unable to be divided

---

prefix

base

suffix

irreversible

means

unable to be reversed or to be restored

---

prefix

base

suffix

irreparable

means

not able to be repaired

---

prefix

base

suffix

inexcusable

means

not able to be excused or forgiven

Blank Graphic Organizer

Building Blocks

Writing

prefix

base

suffix

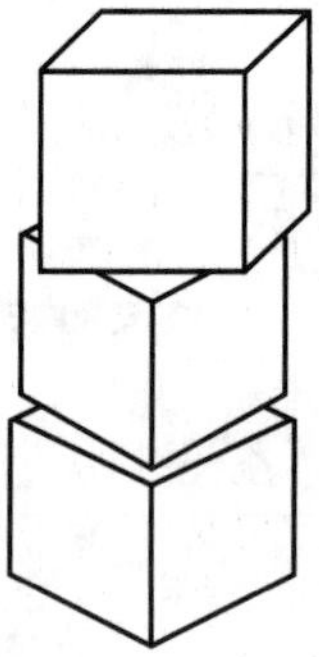

means

_____

prefix

base

suffix

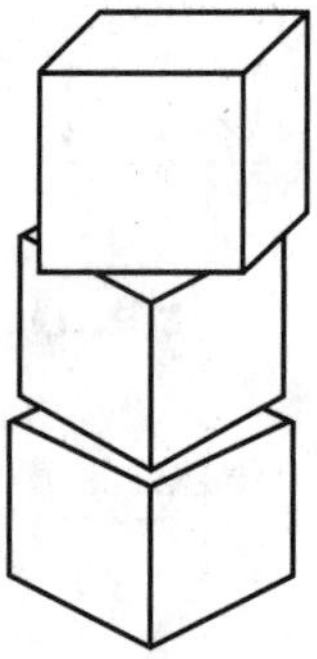

means

_____

prefix

base

suffix

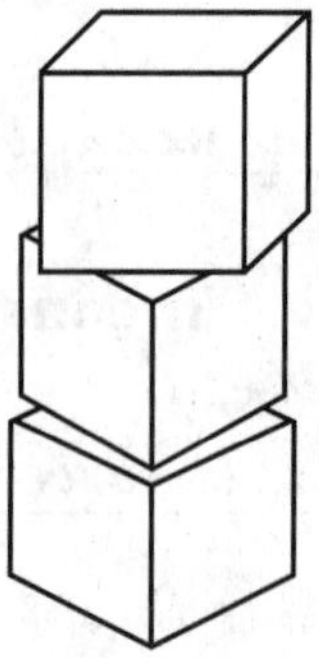

means

_____

prefix

base

suffix

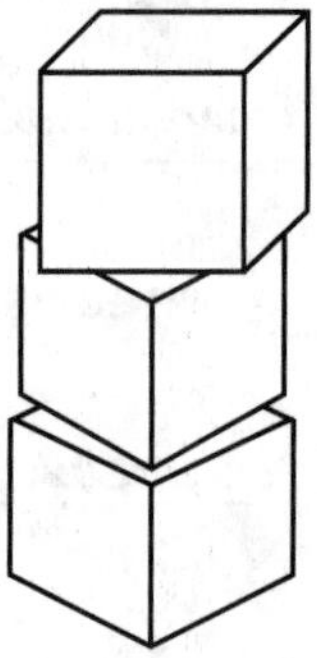

means

_____